Beth Philson
CPO 934

D0822426

Working with
Volunteer
Leaders
in the Church

Working with Volunteer Leaders in the Church

Reginald M. McDonough

BROADMAN PRESS
Nashville, Tennessee

© Copyright 1976 • Broadman Press
All rights reserved

4232-14
ISBN: 0-8054-3214-0

Dewey Decimal Classification: 254
Subject Headings: CHURCH WORK // LEADERSHIP

Library of Congress Card Catalog Number: 75-16579
Printed in the United States of America

To Joan, Mike, and Teri
Three volunteers whom I love very much

Foreword

Working with Volunteer Leaders in the Church is a superb book. It is a practical resource that can become an invaluable tool for use in both small and large churches. The content is extremely practical and provides how-to-do-it help for the most experienced leader or the novice working with volunteers for the first time. Underlying the practical side is a sound administrative theory that pervades and undergirds the entire book.

Many persons give lip-service to the fact that human resources are a leader's most valuable asset. In practice, however, working with and through people does not always take priority.

McDonough writes out of years of personal experience in local churches and denominational work. He ably practices what he advocates. This book has grown out of the day-to-day practical approach that McDonough takes to his own work.

Working with volunteers is a skill that requires study and practice. This book covers the full range of skills that must be mastered. Helpful ideas are presented for finding and enlisting volunteer workers—one of the toughest parts of the job. One of the most enlightening sections deals with reasons why persons volunteer in the first place. I wish that I had known these reasons years ago as I struggled with this job that is akin to building a fence out of warped boards. And worker climate can change so rapidly and seemingly without cause. McDonough explains why and adds what to do about it.

Principles and practices of sound organization are interpreted. Goal-setting with volunteers is explored. Helps for achieving coordination are set forth in such an understandable way that the reader is tempted to ask, "Now why didn't I think of that?" A highlight is the chapter on supervision. McDonough is one of the finest supervisors I know. We have worked side by side for over ten years and I've watched him under all conditions. Here he shares his skills of supervision.

Working with Volunteer Leaders in the Church will enrich your life. And you will, in turn, strengthen the lives of volunteers with whom you will work through the years ahead.

HOWARD B. FOSHEE
Secretary

Church Administration Department
Sunday School Board

Preface

God has given each church a unique mission to achieve. Within each church he has placed the resources to achieve that mission. But resources are expendable. Once they are used, they cannot be used again. A church must be wise in the use of its resources. The most important resource a church has is the gifts that reside in the lives of its members. The New Testament concept of a church leaves no doubt that "the body" depends on all its "members" to achieve its purpose. The harvest that God could reap if all these gifts were put into service is beyond human imagination.

Effective leadership of pastor and staff is a key factor in improving the quantity and quality of output by a church's volunteer leaders. This book is directed to these pastoral ministries leaders. The philosophical thread that runs throughout the book is a faith that deep within every Christian's heart is a desire to use his talents in Christ's service; that the relationship of pastor, staff, and congregation should be a team relationship in which each person's contribution is important; and that developmental leadership is required to give direction and thrust to the enterprise.

The book is intended to be more than a collection of ideas and processes. It seeks to express a philosophy of leadership in practical terms.

An experience several years ago illustrates the need to define at the outset the term *volunteer leader*. After speaking on the subject "How to Work with Volunteers in the Church," I was seated next to one of the conference participants at lunch. While discussing the conference with my luncheon neighbor, I was surprised to learn that he had expected a discussion of how to work with persons in the church who have volunteered for a church vocation. Somewhat shaken, I determined never to take for granted that the term *volunteer worker* has a common meaning to everyone.

In this book a volunteer leader is a person who is serving in a church-elected leadership position without remuneration. This would include such leaders as Sunday School teachers, department directors, committee members, ushers, Church Training leaders, and many other church-elected positions.

The term *volunteer* also implies that a person has accepted a responsibility by coming forth without external influence. This may or may not be true. More often than not a volunteer leader is recruited to accept the assignment by a personal contact from another individual.

REGINALD M. McDONOUGH

Contents

1
Why Bother with Volunteers?

The great army of lay leaders who give their time and talents to Christian service through church leadership positions makes up a mighty force for God. Without this work force the education, outreach, and ministry programs of churches would be reduced to a token of their present size and significance.

Ironically, the use of volunteer leaders has been called the greatest weakness and the greatest strength of the evangelical church. Because of the nonprofessional nature of lay leaders, an article in one national periodical referred to the Sunday School as "Those Wasted Hours." Some educators have called for the dismissal of volunteer leaders and the employment of a staff of professional church teachers. While the need for more effective volunteer leaders cannot be denied, the involvement of the rank and file of the church in carrying out its work is rooted in the very nature of the church itself.

A Biblical Mandate

The New Testament makes it clear that every Christian is to apply his gifts in the pursuit of the Christian mission. William E. Hull states, "The most conspicuous feature of the concept of the Christian priesthood in the New Testament is its radical transformation of the counterpart concept of the Israelite priesthood in the Old Testament." [1]

9

In the Old Testament the priestly duties were limited to the tribe of Levi. In the New Testament the priestly functions were the responsibility of the entire church. Perhaps the most familiar Scripture passage relating to the New Testament concept of the priesthood of all believers is 1 Peter 2:9, "But you are a chosen race, a royal priesthood, a holy nation, God's own people, that you may declare the wonderful deeds of him who called you out of darkness into his marvelous light" (RSV). This verse indicates that the work of the church is not the responsibility of a chosen few but of every one of God's people.

Ephesians 4:16 also strongly teaches the involvement of every Christian in the life and work of the church. In this verse, the apostle Paul compares the church to a body. In *The Living Bible* it reads as follows: "Under his direction the whole body is fitted together perfectly, and each part in its own special way helps the other parts, so that the whole body is healthy and growing and full of love." This Scripture indicates the peculiar nature of each church member's responsibility. Christ is pictured as the head of the church with its members performing the various functions of the body.

A Christian's occupation may be secular, but his vocation is Christian service. These biblical mandates add a sacred dimension to the work of volunteer leaders in the church.

A Practical Necessity

The use of volunteer leadership is not only a biblical mandate but also a practical necessity.

A look at the Shelby Avenue Church will illustrate the dependence of a typical church on its volunteer leaders. This congregation has about six hundred resident members. The employed staff consists of the pastor, a part-time educational director, a part-time music director, a secretary, and a custodian. The church has an age-graded Sunday School on Sunday morning and an age-graded Church Training program on Sunday evening. In addition to the weekly Sunday morning, Sunday evening, and Wednesday evening worship services, a children's worship is conducted on Sunday morning. The church has a women's and girls' missionary organization meeting monthly and a men's and boys' missionary organization that meets quarterly. The church has fifteen church committees, sixteen deacons, and several church officers. All of the church organizations are manned by volunteer leaders.

The volunteer leadership force is organized as follows:

Sunday School	60
Church Training	15
Children's worship	10
Committees	54
Church officers (clerk, treasurer, etc.)	8
Deacons	16
Ushers	8
Women's and men's mission organizations	12
Total	183

The ratio of church-elected, volunteer positions to leadership staff positions is twenty to one. This illustrates the importance and dependence of the Shelby Avenue Church on its volunteer leaders. The church could not operate its present programs with its limited staff.

Several other facts about the volunteer work force of this church are noteworthy. Eighty-six people man the 183 positions—an average of 2.2 positions per leader. Thirty-one are men, and fifty-five are women. Fourteen are under twenty-five years of age, and ten are older than sixty.

Although few if any churches are exactly like it, the Shelby Avenue Church is typical in its overwhelming dependence on volunteer leaders to do its work. It also illustrates the practical necessity of using volunteer leadership to man the numerous organizations of a typical church.

God has placed in every church the creativity and resources needed to achieve its mission. This reservoir of God-given talent resides in all the membership, not just the employed staff. As enablers it is incumbent on the ministers to help church members identify their gifts and apply them in service. To seek to accomplish the church's mission without the full use of its resources is like trying to accomplish a mission with hands and feet tied. The magnitude of a church's mission is such that it must use all of its creativity and resources in the best possible way.

Why Persons Serve as Volunteers

Persons serve in volunteer church positions for many reasons. In fact it is seldom that a single reason provides the motivation for a person's service. More often a combination of motives, some perhaps more noble than others, form the basis for accepting and carrying out a church job.

Paul Veith, a noted author in the field of religious education, lists a variety of motivators for volunteer service:

> There are, no doubt, many reasons which motivate people to render volunteer service—some high, some low. It seems, however, that adequate motivation for service in Christian education is that of the need and the opportunity, which should make an adequate appeal to every loyal church member. This major motivation may be supplemented by such things as a wholesome fellowship of the workers in Christian education, recognition on

the part of the church, provision for attractive working conditions, a dignified and personal invitation from the church, indicating the ground on which this particular individual has been chosen.[2]

Again, volunteering does not necessarily mean to step forward without any outside influence. Normally, a person accepts a volunteer leadership position because of some trigger event. The event may be a request from a friend, a contact by a committee member, or a response to a public appeal. This should not diminish the concept of a person's serving because of divine call. On the contrary, it should cause the ministerial staff to feel keenly the responsibility of creating a climate in which a person can respond to the Holy Spirit's leadership.

A brief explanation of some of the motives and needs that prompt persons to accept a volunteer church position will be given in the following paragraphs. This will serve as a base for delving into more specific and concrete ideas in later chapters.

To Serve Others

Service to fellowman is a central theme in Christianity. Service gives a person a way to put his concerns into action. A team of researchers at The Sunday School Board of the Southern Baptist Convention completed in 1966 the research project "Adult Leadership in Southern Baptist Churches." [3] Its purpose was to provide more detailed and accurate information about the characteristics, beliefs, attitudes, training, and practices of leaders in Southern Baptist churches.

One question on the questionnaire related specifically to the reasons volunteer leaders accepted their responsibilities. The question was, "Why did you accept this position of leadership in your church?" Respondents were asked to check one to three of the choices listed and/or specify the reasons.

The study included a sample of 11,458 leaders from 427 churches. The usable response was 5,396 or 47.1 percent.

The following is a general summary of the response:

Answer	Percent Giving
Felt God's call to this work.	17.6
Want to help others learn of God, Christ, Holy Spirit, and Bible.	15.9
My obligation to witness and spread the gospel.	6.9
Want to guide others to everyday Christian living.	5.4
Teachers or leaders are needed; felt I should help.	5.3

The need to help others was rated second only to a feeling of God's call. To love people and want to help them is certainly a worthy, Christlike motive. Helping people is a legitimate way to live out a person's Christian calling.

On the negative side, however, some persons want to help others because of a sense of guilt. Service to others becomes a way to pay a debt to society or to God for some mistake for which they feel responsible. These persons may feel that God will punish them if they do not serve others. A minister should be sensitive to persons who serve because of guilt and help them to work through their misery to discover the real joy that comes from service aimed at growing people.

In David O. Moberg's book *The Church as a Social Institution,* Wayne Oates has the following comment about service because of guilt:

> Volunteers for teaching assignments and other youth leadership positions often include those least capable to take such respon-

sibility. Many inner needs of such persons are met by religious service. Among them release of guilt, relief from boredom, and escape from family tension. Volunteers are sometimes selfishly grasping for solutions to their own problems, subconsciously subordinating the church's welfare to their own personal needs.[4]

To Gain Love and Acceptance

Persons also accept volunteer positions because of their need to be accepted and loved by other persons. This need to belong is a normal social desire that exists in every healthy person. It is certainly not wrong to want to be involved in a group that can accept you as a person of worth, share your concerns, and help you weather the anxieties and frustrations of life.

In a public affairs pamphlet entitled *What Makes a Volunteer,* Melvin Glasser explains the relationship of belonging to the need to participate in volunteer service:

> Volunteer service answers the need to belong that each of us has—the need to become associated with others in achieving some tangible goal. In many jobs a man works on a part of something, or is a "specialist" in something. He may never see the whole job or the completed job. He feels the need to belong to a group of people with similar interests to accomplish something he can see, to achieve satisfaction in a completed job. Volunteer service can be an answer to this need. For women, too, volunteer service helps to answer the need to belong to some group outside the family. Many women whose children are grown find volunteer work an antidote to feelings of emptiness and loneliness.
>
> Family units in the United States today are almost 40 percent smaller than in 1900 when the average household had five and one-half members. Now it has three and one-half members. This decrease is due to the fewer children and to the fact that there is no longer a place in the household for several relatives. Once the grandparents, widowed relatives, and maiden aunts lived with the family and helped with the work. The family produced much of what it consumed and found much good social and recreational satisfaction in its own large circle. Today's family members must

> seek some of this work in play satisfaction elsewhere. Many find
> their answer in volunteer services where they can share in group
> experiences.[5]

Unfortunately, the need to belong to a group can become a
dominating need in a person's life and cause him to accept responsibilities for which he is not capable. A person feels that
he will be rejected by his friends if he doesn't say yes.

In *The Volunteers* David Sills reports: "The role relationship
most frequently employed in recruiting is that of friendship: 58
percent of all volunteers who were recruited into the Foundation
[March of Dimes] were asked by a friend. This is perfectly in
accord with the conclusions reached in several studies of how
people are influenced—what to buy, what to think about publications, what entertainment to seek, whom to vote for—all have
been shown to be decisions in which personal influence plays
a very large part." [6]

To Obtain Recognition and Status

The fact that some persons accept church leadership positions
to achieve recognition and status is both good and bad. It is good
because God has placed within each person the gifts that he expects
to be used. To desire a platform for the stewardship of these
gifts is commendable. A person with the gift of teaching should
have a desire for a position in which he can use the gift for the
Lord.

On the other hand, a person who accepts a position to advance
his status or power in the church or community is doing himself
and the church a great disservice. It is this type of hypocrisy
that makes a church suspect to persons in the community who
see through the sham.

Other persons accept church leadership positions because of

their deep-felt need for recognition. In many instances recognition may not be possible for them in other areas of their lives. They may be starving for someone to say, "Well done." The ministry of affirmation is a significant responsibility for every leader.

More times than not, a person who accepts or seeks a church position to gain personal status or recognition does so with no feeling of guilt. He rationalizes the situation by saying "I'm getting no more than I deserve," "I'm giving more than I'm getting," or "I'm using my position to benefit the church."

Regardless of the rationalization, accepting a church position to gain personal status and recognition is a page taken from Satan's "playbook."

To Find Self-Fulfillment

Accepting a church leadership position to obtain a sense of accomplishment from achieving a short- or long-term goal is a highly desirable motive. A person who has self-fulfillment as a motive obtains satisfaction from putting into practice the talents and skills he possesses. Persons who serve because of this motive might say: "God has given me a gift to teach. It is a thrilling experience for me. I love to see people grow." Fortunately there are many church leaders who sincerely feel this way. They have a sense of mission about their work. Rather than service being a burden, it is a joy.

Because it is normal for each volunteer leader also to have belonging and ego needs, the need for fulfillment is often expressed in connection with one of these needs. And as the strength of these needs varies from day to day, the quality of the motivation also varies. But fortunately there are many volunteer leaders in the church who feel a sense of mission, joy, and fulfillment in their work.

To Serve God

The previously mentioned Sunday School Board research project in adult leadership reported that the number one reason given by volunteer church leaders for their service was to serve God. Service to God is vital to everyone who feels a debt of gratitude for God's work in his life. This overwhelming motivation cuts across the other reasons that have been given. To serve others is to serve God. To see a position as an opportunity for influence is a service to God. And certainly to fulfill a divine mission is to serve God. The apostle Paul said, "I press toward the mark for the prize of the high calling"; "the love of Christ constraineth us."

Every Christian is grateful to God for his love and redemption. Belonging, recognition, status, and fulfillment needs are God-given. God can work through these needs to lead individuals to accept and faithfully carry out his will.

2
Finding and Enlisting Volunteers

At the height of a discussion about enlistment, invariably someone will ask, "Are we trying to fill positions or help persons discover their gifts and apply them in God's work?" Why can't the two concepts jibe? The church, as a corporate body, is trying to implement the education, evangelism, worship, and ministry programs that will achieve the church's mission. This requires manpower. God has placed within each church the gifts and resources needed to accomplish the mission. The question is not gifts versus filling positions. Both concepts are important and legitimate. If a class of young boys does not have a teacher, one needs to be found. However, only a person who has the necessary gifts and is willing to take the growth of these boys as his mission should be enlisted to take the class. Most persons agree with this concept but too often are willing to compromise when a position goes unfilled for a few weeks.

Eva Schindler-Rainman and Ronald Lippett describe the relationship of gifts and enlistments as a linkage process: "The recruitment process is actually a linkage-process, linking a person who wants to give of himself with an organization that needs volunteers in order to operate; linking a need for self-actualization with an opportunity for experience; linking a need to learn with opportunities for learning; linking a need to be creative with an opportunity to give the most creative service possible." [7]

This chapter will approach enlistment from the perspective of finding and enlisting persons who are qualified and committed to living out their Christian calling in a church-elected leadership position.

Forecasting Volunteer Leadership Needs

The process of enlistment should be well planned. It should begin with a study of the leadership needs of a church.

The study should be two-fold. First, determine the present and future priorities the church must establish to achieve its mission. Leadership is one of only four resources—leaders, time, money, and facilities—that a church has to do its work. Leadership should be placed according to the priority mission of the church. A church whose priority is to reach the college community must see that capable leaders are elected to lead this work. Too many churches make no effort to parallel their enlistment priorities with their program priorities. Too often the enlistment priority is to fill the roster with capable people without giving due attention to program priorities. Before the nominating committee does its work, discuss with them the church's long-range plans and program priorities.

The second part of the study should be a forecast of leadership needs. This forecast is based on the present organizational structure. However, it should reflect changes in the structure that are projected because of anticipated program and enrollment changes. It should pinpoint the number and types of leaders that will be needed at the beginning of each of the next three years. The forecast will serve as a basis for designing the church's pre-service training plan.

The following procedure is one way to complete a leadership forecast. Duplicate the work sheet form illustrated in Figure 1

Figure 1. FORECASTING VOLUNTEER LEADERSHIP REQUIREMENTS

Program Organization:_____

Age Groups and Divisions	Present Enrollments	Present No. of Workers	Ratio of Workers to Enrollment	Projected Enrollment 19__	Projected Enrollment 19__	Projected Enrollment 19__	Desirable Ratio of Workers to Enrollments	Immediate Worker Needs	Projected Number of Workers 19__	Projected Number of Workers 19__	Projected Number of Workers 19__	Average Yearly Turnover	Additional Leadership Requirements 19__	Additional Leadership Requirements 19__	Additional Leadership Requirements 19__
PRESCHOOL															
CHILDREN (6 – 11)															
YOUTH (12–17)															
YOUNG ADULT (18–29)															
ADULTS (30–59)															
SENIOR ADULTS (60—UP)															
SPECIAL GROUPS															

to use as a guide. Since the Sunday School organization normally requires the largest number of workers, begin with it.

To get ready, record the organization on the work sheet. Then enter the age divisions and the present enrollment and number of workers in each. Use the following seven steps to complete the forecast.

1. *Determine the desirable leader/pupil ratio.*—One to ten can be used as an across-the-board figure, but for the forecast it will be more helpful to select a specific figure for each age group. For example, a special education class for children would require more workers per child than a young adult department. If you are not sure what the best ratio would be, check a reliable resource or a knowledgeable leader.

2. *Calculate present needs.*—Check the present leader/pupil ratio. How does it compare with the desirable ratio? There may be some areas where you are not presently meeting your expectations. The shortages should be included in the big picture.

3. *Project the enrollment for at least the next three years.*—To do this accurately, examine at least three sources:
- *The growth or decline of the various groups in recent years*
- *Community trends*
- *Church plans for strategic advance*

4. *Figure the number of leaders that will be needed to staff each year's enrollment.*—Use the leader/pupil ratio that was determined in step 1.

5. *Check the turnover.*—Turnover is a major factor of leadership forecasting. It may be a shock to realize the rate of turnover. Turnover should include those who do not "reenlist" at the end of the year as well as those who resign during the year.

6. *Put it all together.*—Add to the number of leaders needed for each of the years the average turnover expected. Subtract

the present number of leaders, and the forecast of new leaders is complete.

   7. One more step.—Think through the type of leaders that will be needed. If your projection calls for additional departments, some of the leaders will need to be department directors. Also, try to anticipate where you will find the leaders. Will they be shifted from other age groups or will persons who are not serving be enlisted?

Discovering Potential Leaders

   It is my conviction that the leadership skills needed to accomplish a church's mission can be found within its membership. This is a difficult conviction to live by because I know of no church that has all the leaders it could use effectively. But God will not give a mission if the resources are not available to accomplish it. The challenge is to discover the gifts and other resources God has placed in the membership and link them together effectively.

   This first step of an enlistment process is to set up a discovery system that will facilitate a match-up of the gifts and interests of persons with the leadership needs of the church's program.

Investigate Multiple Sources

   Locating church members with the skills and interests needed to fill positions is hard work. The most frequent shortcoming of a minister or nominating committee is to consider only persons who come to mind. It is amazing how many persons will be overlooked by making a list through a series of mental gymnastics only.

   Many sources can and should be used to find potential leaders. Here are some possibilities:

1. The church roll
2. Adults and older youth in Church Training
3. Vacation Bible School faculty
4. New church members
5. Returning college students
6. Returning servicemen and women
7. Persons attending training conferences and conventions
8. Associate officers and substitute teachers
9. Persons who have completed training courses
10. Persons included in talent files
11. Schoolteachers and administrators
12. Businessmen and women whose work requires group leadership
13. Retired persons
14. Church members who are leaders in community affairs
15. Persons who have previously served as teachers and officers
16. Information on letters of recommendations from other churches
17. Potential leader classes
18. Recommendations from present teachers and officers
19. Recommendations from deacons regarding their membership group
20. Visitation contacts

Deal with Total Possibilities

It is important to deal with total possibilities. Todd Hamilton, now missionary to the Philippines, suggests a practical way to do this. This idea has been used successfully to enlist Vacation Bible School leaders.

1. Write the name, address, and phone number of every church member who is a potential VBS leader on a separate 3 by 5

card. Use the church roll to do this. Don't leave anyone out unless he works at the time of the school or is an inactive member. Sometimes persons who have conflicting work hours will even take some of their vacation time. This is particularly true of individuals who may have four to six weeks vacation. The list may be made from the addressing machine file if the church has one.

2. Enlist the department directors and tell them that they cannot contact anyone to work in their departments until after a worker assignment meeting.

3. Divide the 3 by 5 cards into six stacks according to which age division you think each person would serve—Preschool, younger Children, older Children, Youth, Adult, and unknown.

4. Conduct an assignment meeting with the department directors. Prepare a large chalkboard with a square for each department you expect to have. Begin by going through your stack of prospective Preschool workers. When a name is called, the card may be claimed by one of the department directors or returned to the stack. When a card is claimed, write the prospective leader's name in the appropriate square. When each Preschool director has two more than the number of leaders needed, move over to the younger Children. Continue until all directors have a list of persons to contact.

5. Instruct the directors to contact you in person or by phone for additional names if they do not secure enough leaders from their contacts. As other names are taken, pass the cards to the directors.

By this system, the better leaders can be distributed among the various departments. If one director begins to get more of the capable persons on his list, give the other directors first choice until the situation has balanced out.

The system can also be used by the nominating committee to staff the church program organizations.

Establish a Skill and Interest File

To establish a file of members' experience, skills, and interests is an old but reliable part of a discovery system. The file serves as a reservoir of information that can be used in the enlistment process.

The information for the file can be gathered in various ways. A survey can be taken through church organizations, at church services, by direct mail, or in a combination of these ways.

A Christian service card illustrated in Figure 2 may be obtained from most Christian book stores.

The file should be arranged alphabetically by family name. If more than fifty cards are in the file, some method of flagging or punching them for quick sorting will be needed. Multicolored metal or plastic tabs may be purchased at an office supply store. Each color can represent some type of information. However, since the tabs make the cards thicker at the top than the bottom, a file of several hundred cards is often difficult to handle.

Another method is to punch holes around the edge of the cards to represent various items listed on them. Then notch the holes for items you wish to flag on a card. By running a knitting needle through a particular hole and shaking the stack of cards, the cards with that particular hole clipped out will fall out of the stack. Prepunched cards may be obtained from Kader Specialities Publisher, 1389 Highland Drive, Clearwater, Florida 33516.

Office equipment companies also have visible index files that can be used. These cards lie flat in a tray with the edge showing. Usually colored plastic tabs are used to flag the designated items. Office supply companies will have information about these systems.

CHRISTIAN SERVICE SURVEY

MR.
MRS.
MISS

Residence _____ Phone _____ Single ☐; Married ☐

Business Address _____ Phone _____ Date _____

Birth date: Month _____ day _____ year _____ ; Education: Grammar School ☐; High School ☐; College ☐

Have Served	Will Serve	SUNDAY SCHOOL	Age Group
		Superintendent	
		Teacher	
		V.B.S.	

Have Served	Will Serve	TRAINING UNION	Age Group
		Director	
		Leader	
		Sponsor	
		Counselor	

Have Served	Will Serve	MUSIC MINISTRY
		Choir: Voice Part _____
		Instrument Played _____
		Song Leader
		Help with Graded Choirs Age Group _____

Have Served	Will Serve	W.M.U.
		Officer
		Sunbeam Worker
		G.A. Worker
		Y.W.A. Worker

Have Served	Will Serve	BROTHERHOOD
		Officer
		R.A. Counselor

I am a	GENERAL AREA
	Tither
	Deacon
	Ordained Minister
	Nurse: Reg. ☐; Prac. ☐
	Blood Donor: Type _____

LIST OTHER INTERESTS ON BACK; CHECK HERE ☐

I will assist in:

	Audio-Visual Aids
	Dramatics
	Flower Arranging
	Food Service
	Handcrafts
	Library Work
	Mission Work
	Photography
	Poster Making
	Recreation
	Soul Winning
	Telephoning
	Transportation
	Typing-Office Work
	Ushering
	Visitation

Code 436-652, Form 100, Broadman Supplies, Nashville, Tenn., Printed in U.S.A.

Figure 2

Contract with Broadman System '70

Broadman System '70 is a church records service that uses the speed and efficiency of electronic data processing to store and retrieve information. The service has been available since the early 70's. It was designed by specialists in the EDP field with the advice of pastors, ministers of education, church business administrators, and secretaries.

The master membership profile is the heart of the system. This profile uses an input card that is completed by every church member. The completed card includes information about an individual's membership in church organizations, his skills, leadership experience, and interests. This information is stored in a computer. Lists of individuals grouped according to the characteristic desired can be retrieved from the computer. For example, a list can be obtained of all the women who have worked with children in grades 4-6 in Sunday School. The lists can be printed out on pressure sensitive labels or standard printout sheets. Churches interested in more information about the system should write Broadman System '70, P. O. Box 2130, Irving, Texas 75060.

Enlisting Volunteer Leaders

After a list of potential leaders has been developed come the crucial tasks of selecting the person to be contacted, making the contact, and securing a commitment to serve.

Create a Climate

The apostle Paul uses the body as analogy of the way all church members should contribute to the work of the church. However, this concept has not been accepted and applied. Some Christians may feel like babes in Christ and unworthy to hold a leadership position. Others may fail to see the wide variety of leadership opportunities that are available. Other Christians may not be serving because of sin in their lives. They know the needs and have ability but will not respond because of the cost of discipleship. Some persons may not respond because they simply are not aware of the needs. Some persons hesitate because of a lack of self-confidence. These persons need assurance and training. Some are not serving because they have not been asked.

Regardless of the reason, it is helpful to seek to build a climate in which the Holy Spirit can guide a person to consider his gifts and consecrate them to service.

Many methods can be used such as sermons, bulletin boards, dedication services, articles in the church newsletter, special programs in department periods, and studies in Sunday School and church membership training.

One church tied all of its efforts together under the theme "Life's Greatest Adventure." The pastor preached a series of sermons on commitment to service. Posters, bulletin boards, and banners were placed around the church. The month-long emphasis was climaxed with a dedication service where members pledged their service.

Selecting the Person

What qualifications should be met by persons holding church leadership positions? Each church should determine the qualification which it desires for the type of work required.

The pamphlet *The Nominating Committee* gives four areas of qualification that should be considered.

1. *Church membership*—persons filling leadership positions in a church should be members of the church. They should be actively involved in the life of the church and demonstrate a commit-

ment to and concern for the work of Christ.

2. *Aptitude*—church leaders should demonstrate aptitude for the work in which they are asked to lead. Genuine interest, flexibility, creativity, initiative, and a sense of purpose are highly desirable characteristics also.

3. *Performance*—church leaders should demonstrate dependability and responsibility in tasks assigned to them by the church.

4. *Experience*—certain specialized leadership positions require special understandings and experience. These factors should be considered to the degree that they apply to each position.[8]

The minister or nominating committee should choose the person they feel is best qualified for each position. The church's priorities, a person's qualifications and attitude, and the Holy Spirit's leadership must influence this choice. This decision should be made with the involvement of the person who is to be the chosen individual's supervisor. For example, the Sunday School director should participate in the selection of the person who will be asked to be department director.

Making the Contact

When approval has been obtained from the nominating committee, the person who will supervise the leader should make the enlistment contact. For example, the Sunday School director should contact the department director. The department director should contact the teachers. This enables the supervisor to tell the person what will be expected of him. If the nominating committee does all the enlisting, the job expectation may not be explained properly. Also, the nominating committee may be so anxious to complete their assignment that a committee member may play down the demands of the job and compromise the qualifications. As a staff member, you may accompany the supervisor and help in the interview, but always make sure the supervisor is involved. If you do the enlisting, the person will feel responsible to you and not his supervisor.

A personal visit is the most effective method of enlistment. A personal visit shows the importance of the job. It gives opportunity for verbal and nonverbal communication. A public appeal is not out of the question although it is certainly less effective. A person may come forward who is not qualified. However, God sometimes impresses qualified persons to volunteer—people whom our most conscientious discovery process has missed.

Again, the pamphlet *The Nominating Committee* gives several good suggestions for making the personal visit:

1. Make an appointment—either call or personally set a time for discussion.
2. Prepare for the interview with prayer.
3. Be positive about the opportunity for service or do not go.
4. Have available materials the prospective leader will need for the work.
5. Give all the information about the assignment—its problems and its opportunities.
6. Discuss training and planning helps the church offers.
7. Seek a prayerful decision. Be prepared to accept the yes and yet allow for more time, if time will be of help.
8. If yes is the answer, schedule appropriate training for the new worker. If no is the answer, express appreciation for the time spent in consideration and encourage the worker to seek some kind of potential leader-training experience.[9]

Using the Nominating Committee Effectively

The principal function of the nominating committee is to lead in staffing all church-elected volunteer leadership positions. It should consist of five to seven members elected at large. Its specific responsibilities are:

1. Select, interview, and enlist church program organization leaders, church program service leaders, church committee chairmen, and general officers.

2. Screen volunteer workers before they are invited to serve in church-elected leadership positions. The program organization and services leaders and committee chairmen will be enlisting workers to serve in leadership positions. The workers should be screened by the nominating committee before the program leaders or committee chairmen enlist them.

3. Distribute church leadership according to priority needs. Leadership is like money or any other resource of the church. It needs to be budgeted. Leaders should be placed where their talents can best be used to move the church toward the accomplishment of its mission.

4. Assist church leaders in discovering and enlisting qualified persons to fill church-elected positions of leadership in their respective organizations. The nominating committee should serve as a source from which the program leaders and committee chairmen can be of assistance in discovering potential workers. The nominating committee should encourage leaders to enlist the workers they will guide. However, the committee should be ready to give any assistance that may be needed.

5. Present volunteer workers to the church for election. The nominating committee is responsible for nominating workers to the church for official election.

6. Nominate special committees as assigned by the church, such

as a constitution committee. The use of one nominating committee should give a better balance and wider distribution of work among the members. A committee on committees, separate from the nominating committee, will likely cause a duplication of effort.

Serve as a Clearing House

In many churches the nominating committee makes all the enlistment contacts for volunteer workers. For the reasons given earlier, with the exception of the heads of the organizations, the enlistment visits should be made by the supervising leader. A major role of the nominating committee should be to see that the church's leadership resources are placed in accord with the priorities. As duty No. 3 states, the nominating committee should budget the church's leadership. Before persons are contacted, they should be approved by the nominating committee.

Make Organization Directors Ex Officio

Many churches automatically add the organization directors to the nominating committee when the director is elected. This practice burdens the nominating committee and keeps them from operating effectively year round. Because organization directors must give priority to the leadership of their congregations, they have difficulty finding time to give to the nominating committee. By making these leaders ex officio, they can attend the committee meetings only when necessary. When they are present, they can vote.

Function Year-Round

The nominating committee should be a regular committee that works year-round to staff vacancies and prepare for the next enlistment cycle. The committee should begin enlisting program directors at least five months before the new church year begins. If the church year begins in October, the committee should present the program directors to the church in the May through June church business conference. The new roster should be complete in time for pre-service orientation and training.

Distribute the Work Load

Twenty percent of the church members usually do eighty percent of the work. A church needs a plan to seek a broader distribution of the work load. It is easy to relinquish and enlist the faithful few to do most of the work.

Many churches have a policy that no person can hold two major responsibilities. These major responsibilities are usually directors, teachers, and committee chairman.

Some churches have even developed a point system to rate each position. Each volunteer leader's point total must fall below the maximum allowed one person.

Consider Three-Year Enlistment

Many hours are spent each year in the enlistment process. Also, a one-year term of service limits the amount of training a person can take. For years, churches have used a three-year enlistment plan for committee members. Why not do the same for volunteer directors and teachers? An annual review would be needed. Natural attrition and the immediate filling of the vacancies will prevent all the terms from ending in the same year.

A few churches have established an indefinite enlistment plan with an annual review. The leaders in these churches say the major difference between this approach and annual reenlistment is the necessity of dealing with problems when they occur rather than waiting until the next cycle. The problems can't be put off until the first of the next church year.

To paint a picture requires many strokes. Each stroke must relate to and complement the other. So it is with finding and enlisting volunteer leaders. An organization cannot rise above the quality of its leadership. The effective linking of the gifts and goals of individual Christians with the needs and missions of a church is absolutely essential to the success of the enterprise. Effective enlistment is only one step toward effective work. Training, motivation, and supervision are also needed.

3
Developing an Effective Training Plan

"Train, Retrain, Reeducate, or Die!" This slogan is said to be printed over a door through which the American astronauts pass as they prepare for space flight. It is a grim reminder that to fail to prepare is to prepare to fail.

Without trained leaders an endeavor has two strikes against it before it starts. The quality of work that a person can do is directly linked to his preparation for the task. Some workers bring a background of experience to their jobs and need little basic training. Their need is for advanced, in-service training to help them continue to grow as they serve. Other persons have little experience or training. Their reason for accepting a particular job is their concern for needs, and their commitment. Both pre-service and in-service training are needed to help them become effective volunteer leaders. Regardless of the type of training needed, every worker can see more results from his work if he is continually involved in meaningful development activities. Every church needs a leader training plan that is comprehensive and geared to the felt needs of its program and workers.

Organizing for Leader Training

Leader training is so important it should not be left to sporadic efforts on an "as needed" basis. A definite, continuing organization is needed to determine leader training needs and administer a comprehensive leader training program. Some churches refer to the organization as a leader training department. This can be a limiting view if it is conceived to be like a Sunday School department that meets only at a certain time and place. A church leader training department must meet throughout the week in various locations. Whether the enterprise is called a church leader department or church leader training program, officers will be needed.

Director of Church Leader Training

The first step toward an effective leader training program is the election of a director of church leader training. This person should serve as a general officer in the Church Training program and Sunday School. If a church has a minister of education, he may serve in this capacity. However, if a capable layman can be enlisted, the minister of education can multiply his own efforts by serving in tandem with the layman. The director of church leader training should meet often with the church council and may be a member of the council. His work is primarily administrative rather than instructive. His specific duties are:

1. Determine the leadership training needs of the church
2. Discover persons for training as leaders
3. Enlist persons in training
4. Decide how training can best be accomplished
5. Schedule training activities
6. Select capable instructors and prepare them for training assignments
7. Keep leader training activities before the church
8. Provide training for leaders of special church projects and/or emphases
9. Recognize training accomplishments

10. Assist the nominating committee and the leaders of church organizations in putting persons to work who have completed training.[10]

Instructors

A church leader training director who also tries to lead most of the training events will find it very difficult to develop a comprehensive leader training program. He simply will not have enough time to administer the program and lead the training events. Capable instructors should be enlisted to conduct training events. The instructor's duties are:

1. Assist the director to develop the content for training events
2. Conduct training events as assigned courses
3. Assist in the enlistment of trainees if appropriate
4. Evaluate trainee response and recommend further training
5. Assist the director with administrative duties as agreed

The selection of instructors is important. The quality of the training events will be no better than the quality of instruction. Also, trainees will be much easier to enlist if the reputation of the instructor is one of excellence.

Some instructors may be regular members of the church leader training staff. These persons would likely lead basic pre-service training courses. Special instructors should be enlisted for specialized pre-service and in-service events. These persons may be members of the church, or they may be outside specialists. For example, if a study of youth teaching methods is needed, the church may have a capable and respected youth leader who can lead the study. However, an outside specialist from another church or a denominational agency may be engaged.

Surveying Types of Training

Although a leader training program should be designed according to the specific needs of a church's programs and leaders, a comprehensive leader training program should have progressive stages of development. The program should include potential leader training, pre-service job training, and in-service training.

Potential Leader Training

The purpose of potential leadership training is to help older youth and adults identify their gifts and interests, learn general leadership skills, survey the work of the church, and determine where they feel God is leading them to begin their leadership pilgrimage.

This type of training is generally offered in two ways. First, many of the general church membership studies provide potential leader training. Participation in a Bible survey course offered to all church members can prove very valuable as a person later assumes a leadership position. Also, many units of the regular Church Training curriculum prepare a person for leadership.

The second approach to potential leader training is more formal. A weekly course is offered that may be three months, six months, or nine months in duration. All older youth and adults should be encouraged to take the course. However, the size of the group should be limited to twenty persons each time the course is offered. Since the nature of this training is exploratory, each participant should have ample opportunity to participate in group activities and discussion. The instructors should give as much individual attention as possible to each person.

The content of the course may be arranged in the following way:

1. The Call to Service
2. Jesus the Teacher
3. The Place of the Bible in Christian Education
4. Introduction to Leadership
5. The Role of the Teacher/Leader
6. A Survey of Age-divisions
7. A Survey of Church Programs (organizations)
8. Human Relations Skills
9. Group Leadership Skills
10. Developing a Meaningful Devotional Life
11. Understanding Self
12. Assessing Gifts and Interests
13. The Joy of Service

The potential leader training class may meet on Sunday morning, Sunday evening, Wednesday evening, or any combination of these times. Participants should commit themselves to be regular in attendance or wait until a later course. The course should be continually repeated. Persons taking it should be assured beforehand that it is an exploration course. Enlistment does not commit them to accept a leadership position when the course is completed.

Pre-service Basic Job Training

Basic job training is that training required to enable a person to function in a specific leadership role.[11] The term *pre-service* indicates that the training is prior to the date a person begins to function in a particular job. However, this discussion will assume that pre-service training can also occur during the first few months that a person functions in a job.

A person's readiness for training is greatest just after he has agreed to take a specific function and during the first few months of service. The emphasis of this training should be to help the person achieve an adequate level of performance for his job.

In the *Leader Training Handbook,* Jimmy Crowe provides the following outline of content that should be included in basic job training:

1. Learning to use curriculum materials
   (1) How to select materials
   (2) How to survey materials
   (3) How to adapt materials to meet specific needs
   (4) How to use leader's materials
   (5) How to use the Bible with the materials selected
2. Learning to use methods
   (1) How to select appropriate methods
   (2) How to use methods
   (3) How to select and use Bible skill activities
   (4) How to use the Bible in a group session
3. Learning to administer
   (1) How to organize
   (2) How to plan
   (3) How to conduct
   (4) How to evaluate
   (5) How to maintain and use records
   (6) How to enlist
   (7) How to lead others to achieve organizational goals
   (8) How to reflect the Holy Spirit in leadership[12]

A survey of the Bible and church doctrines could be added to this outline, especially if the person will be serving in a Sunday School teaching position.

Pre-service training can be implemented in many ways. A comprehensive and intensive plan is given in *Ideas for Training Sunday School Workers,* William R. Cox, editor. The plan calls for training activities on Sunday morning and Sunday evening for a period of six months.

The course provides training in age-group survey, teaching methods, practice teaching, Bible survey, Bible interpretation, church doctrines, enlargement and witnessing, organization and administration.

An orientation for thirteen weeks is another method of pre-service training that has been used successfully. An orientation can be offered for the new teacher in each age division. The group can meet on Sunday evening or another night during the week. An outline of the content for thirteen sessions might be:

1. The role of a teacher
2. Understanding the needs of persons
3. Church doctrine—part one
4. Church doctrine—part two
5. Principles of Bible interpretation
6. Teacher and pupil resource materials
7. Steps in lesson preparation
8. Selecting an aim
9. Steps in teaching a lesson
10. Teaching methods—part one
11. Teaching methods—part two
12. Class organization and administration
13. Review

A special study during the week preceding the beginning of the new church year is also a successful pre-service training approach that is used annually by many churches. The study is usually called Preparation Week. The study serves a dual purpose of launching and training. It may be a general study with all workers in one group or subdivided by age divisions. The content of the study should depend on the needs of the workers and the program emphasis to be launched.

Individual study is a training method that should not be overlooked. Individual study can be tailored to meet each person's needs.

The disturbing fact about pre-service training is that so little of it is done. Many churches elect a person to a position, give him the curriculum materials, and ask him to meet his new class on the first Sunday of the new church year. It's no wonder that the drop out rate is so high and that the quality of leadership is often below par.

In-service Training

Training is a life-long need. It is estimated that one third of the volunteer leaders resign or change positions after one year of service. Although the high rate of turnover can be attributed to many factors, a lack of continuing development in a job is a major cause. Many workers fear they will run out of ideas and different things to say. One worker was heard to say, "I don't stay in a job but one year. I run out of anything new to say and begin to repeat myself." Continued freshness of content comes from continued training and development.

In-service training has the potential of being very practical because it relates to work that a person is presently doing. If the training is planned according to the felt needs of volunteer leaders, participation should be excellent. A word of caution should be noted, however. Many staff leaders make a serious mistake by planning training that they want the volunteers to have rather than planning events that volunteers feel they need. The most successful and meaningful in-service training is that which makes easier and more effective the nitty-gritty, every-week kinds of jobs that workers must do. Persons are not as interested in studying the principles of learning as they are in knowing how to carry out their assignments next Sunday. The principles of learning and other theoretical content should be taught in the context of the immediate, practical concerns of the volunteer leaders.

The Church Leader Training Handbook offers an outline of content for advanced general leadership which is a good scope statement for this phase of in-service training.

1. *Self-understanding:* Learning to look at himself as a Christian leader, how others see him, what motivates him, how to accept himself, how to evaluate abilities and limitations, and the Holy Spirit in the life of a leader.

2. *Developing understanding of group work:* Learning how groups work and how individuals in groups react and interact, and studying group work from a Christian perspective.

3. *Developing understanding of a program or service* [organization]: Learning the specific tasks of his organization and how these tasks relate to other church organizations.

4. *Developing understanding of age groups or special groups:* Learning characteristics of the age group, the age group's ability to grasp biblical and theological concepts, environment and activities suitable for the age group.

5. *Developing leadership skills:* Learning how to plan and achieve group goals; to give direction to a group; to communicate effectively; to use group involvement, evaluation, motivation, and problem-solving techniques; to delegate, determine priorities, select and use methods; and, to encourage spiritual growth and development.[13]

In addition to these general leadership training areas, in-service training should include Bible study and special program content. For example, a mission action worker should include mission study in his plan of in-service training.

A great variety of methods and approaches can be used to conduct in-service training. Both short-term and extended courses should be included. The most successful program has something scheduled every week. In fact, in the long run more benefit will be gained from small groups meeting regularly throughout the year than from a few big training events.

Harriet Naylor suggests four types of short-term events—a short institute, round table, workshop, and seminar.[14]

1. *A short institute.*—This event is heavily subject oriented and the teaching objectives are related to the currency and importance of the information to the learners. The flow of information tends to be from expert to learners. A great deal of information is transmitted in a short time.

2. *A round table.*—This event is usually centered around common experiences and problems. The group shares workable solutions to common problems. The meeting is usually work-related by a peer. This is a poor way to use an expert but a good way to get interaction among persons in similar jobs.

3. *A workshop.*—This event combines the sharing of subject matter with practice in a selected area. The group may produce a report. Each person contributes to the analysis, planning, and conducting of the project. Practical experience is the unique feature of this type of event. The term *practicum* is also used to describe this type event.

4. *A seminar or conference.*—These terms are used loosely to describe hear-and-discuss-type of events. Seminars are usually longer in duration than conferences. The learning objectives are generally person-centered and job competence is the primary benefit.

Individual study is also an excellent in-service training approach. The booklet *Ideas for Training Sunday School Workers* mentioned earlier presents an individual plan, "A Job Training Plan for Sunday School Leaders." The plan includes a job training guide for each position in a Sunday School organization. The guide is a self-study plan in step-by-step form.

One church conducted a self-study plan "Operation Know." Each quarter a different book or category of books was selected for self-study. The director of church leader training obtained a quantity of books for sale to participants. An "Operation Know" honor roll of those who completed the study was displayed each quarter.

Another successful approach is to conduct a variety of training events for a particular age division each quarter. The specific events should be selected according to the needs of the leaders. This idea makes use of the concept of hit-it-hard for a short period as compared with a more spaced-out approach.

Denominational conferences, seminars, and workshops offer other excellent approaches for in-service training. In addition to the top quality style that usually characterizes these events, the opportunity to share with leaders from other churches gives an added dimension of motivation.

Developing a Training Plan

A part of the annual plan for the church should be a leader training plan. The plan should be an integral part of the church's annual plan but it should also be pulled out for evaluation and control. The director of leader training should be responsible for putting the plan together. If he is not a staff leader, he should obviously develop the plan in conjunction with the staff, church council, and church training council.

Diagnosing Leader Training Needs

In *Diagnosing Leader Training Needs*, Robert Holley suggests five methods of discovery—surveys, observation, records studies, interviews, and questionnaires.[15] Each of these methods is described in the guide.

Four basic questions should be considered:

1. Which leadership positions are currently vacant?
2. How many additional leaders will be needed to staff new work planned for the future and when will they be needed?
3. What are the basic needs of leaders now serving?
4. What special church projects are proposed and what training will workers need to conduct them? [16]

The questionnaire illustrated in Figure 3, may also be used to obtain the opinions of the volunteer leaders.

Figure 3

My Training Needs

1. Rank the following needs in the order of their importance to you. (*1* is most important; *15* is least important)
   _____ Using a variety of methods
   _____ Discovering the needs and interests of others
   _____ Counseling with persons in my group
   _____ Using resource materials
   _____ Planning more effectively
   _____ Involving persons in discussion
   _____ Understanding myself
   _____ Understanding the Bible
   _____ Evaluating results
   _____ Dealing with difficult people
   _____ Enlisting persons
   _____ Managing my time
   _____ Delegating effectively
   _____ Helping others become motivated
   _____ Dealing with absentees

2. Check the study approaches you prefer:
   _____ Self-study
   _____ Sunday evening courses
   _____ Sunday morning courses

_____ Wednesday evening courses
_____ Three evening institutes
_____ Friday evening and Saturday retreats
_____ Saturday all day
_____ Denominational conferences in our city
_____ Denominational conferences at regional conference
          centers

Putting the Plan Together

After the needs have been identified, the leader training plan
should be put into a form which can be shared and evaluated.
Figure 4 illustrates one way that this can be done. The plan should
include the persons to be trained, the major emphasis of the
training, major resources, the form of training, the date, other
events to which the training is related, and the person responsible.
The persons enlisted to lead the training events can be church-
elected instructors in the church leader training department, or
they can be persons with expertise who are enlisted to do a single
event. Be creative in the selection of the schedule. Variety in
location and schedule builds interest.

There are many good things a church can do but there are
some things a church must do if it is to achieve its mission. Training
is one of these priority items. Training is a life or death matter
not only for the astronauts, but also for a church. The only way
a church can have an effective education, outreach, and mission
program is through an effective leader training program. Training
is the number one priority of a staff leader.

Figure 4

Annual Training Plan/Main Street Church

Who Is to Be Trained	Major Emphasis	Major Resources	Form of Training	Timing	Relation to Other Events	Personal Group Responsible
1. Ushers	Orientation, new ushers	Filmstrip, church usher booklet	One evening institute	October	Revival, October	Bill Young
2. Backyard Bible study leaders	Materials, enlistment, methods	Teacher's and pupils' materials	All day Saturday	April	Backyard Bible study emphasis, June	George Moser
3. Potential leaders	Gifts, age-div. survey, skills, expectations	Special notebook	Sunday evening	New class quarterly	None	B. A. Hildreth
4. Adult Sunday teachers	New teaching methods	New book on subject	Friday—Saturday retreat	October 30	Beginning of Adult emphasis in January	Irene Prince
5. Youth teachers and officers	Total-time teaching	Videotape series and workbooks	Four Wednesday evenings	March	Beginning trial, April 1	Naomi Thomas
6. Orientation for new teachers	Survey of duties and skills	Manuals, filmstrips	Five Sunday evenings	September	Beginning work, October 1	Levi Spears

4
Building a Climate for Motivation

Two volunteer leaders, John and Sue, work in the same department. They are supervised by the same department director. At the beginning of the year both are excited about their work. However, after three months John's excitement begins to fade. His attendance at planning meetings becomes irregular. Mary doesn't follow John's pattern. She remains steady and faithful to her responsibility.

Why the difference? They both were exposed to the same training opportunities. Both received similar leadership from the staff and department director. Why does one maintain a high level of motivation and the other fall by the wayside? What can a leader do to help John regain a high level of motivation? What should be done to help Mary maintain her level of motivation?

Obviously there are no simple answers to these questions. However, an understanding of the process and factors in motivation provide some important clues. The basic needs of persons also give insight into the various motivational patterns of individuals.

The Basic Principles of Motivation

A common question asked by leaders is, "How can I motivate my workers?" The answer is that a leader can't. To say that one person can motivate another person is a myth. A person's motivation—low or high—is a product of his will, not the leader's. This is the first principle of motivation. Both internal and external forces have a bearing on a person's motivation, but under normal circumstances the decision to act comes from within each person. A leader can only offer incentives and seek to create a climate in which a person will motivate himself.

A second basic principle is that a person is motivated by his needs. A human is a need-seeking organism. He is pulled by his needs to respond. Man has both primary and secondary needs. Primary needs—such as the need for food and water—are innate. Secondary needs, man's social needs, are learned. Because of the significance of human needs in motivation, the next section of this chapter will give a more complete explanation of man's needs.

A person's behavior is seldom a response to a single need. This is the third basic principle. Man is a complex being and so are his motivations. His behavior is most often motivated by a combination of needs with varying strengths working simultaneously. The eating of food, which is a basic physiological need, is often linked with a social need. Eating may be associated with a person's feeling of rejection or lack of status.

An obvious reason for behavior may be tied to a chain of more subtle reasons. For example, a person may wear high-heeled shoes because the shoes are in style and will help boost his ego. However, the person may also feel inferior because he is short and wear the shoes to bolster his self-esteem. The existence of a needs chain is an important principle for a leader to understand. A leader cannot jump to simplistic conclusions about a person's needs. A leader must also seek to deal with a person as a whole person.

The work of Abraham Maslow in arranging human needs in a hierarchy of relative potency describes a fourth principle of motivation. As illustrated in Figure 5, Maslow arranges human needs in five categories: physiological, safety or security, love

Maslow's Hierarchy of Needs
Figure 5

or belonging, status or ego, and self-actualization.[17] Through his experimentation and study he found that some of these needs are stronger than others. The lower, primary needs, required to exist physically are called the physiological needs. These needs must be satisfied even if other needs go unmet. The relative potency of needs moves from the most basic level to the need of self-actualization, which is the highest category of needs. But while self-actualization is the highest category of needs, it is also the category that a person can most easily leave unfulfilled.

The fifth principle is closely related to the fourth. This principle states that as lower needs are satisfied higher needs have more influence on a person's behavior. Based on this principle, it is no wonder many volunteer leaders do not hear a minister who is appealing to them on the basis of giving themselves to the mission of Christ (self-actualization) when their lower needs are not being satisfied. To look at this principle another way, a satisfied need is no longer a motivator. When a volunteer leader feels that he has been accepted by his peers and has enough status to meet his ego needs, he is capable of responding to the challenge to become self-actualized.

Another principle projected by Maslow is that a growth-oriented process of motivation is superior to a deficit-oriented process. Deficit motivation is a cyclical process as illustrated in Figure 6. First, a need exists. On the basis of this need, a person sets a goal, consciously or subconsciously, that he feels will satisfy the need. Goal-oriented activity is then carried out to satisfy the need. Finally, the need is satisfied. However, when the need recurs, the cycle repeats itself. For example, a person's ego needs may cause him to want a more prestigious leadership position. His goal becomes the achievement of the position. He seeks the position by asking a friend to recommend him to the committee responsible for filling the position. After the recommendation is made and he is asked to take the position, his ego need is temporarily satisfied.

This deficit process of motivation is repeated many times each day in many areas of our lives. It should not be viewed as a necessarily devious or evil process. God created man as a need-oriented being. A problem arises, however, when a person becomes dominated by a deficit process of motivation. An egomaniac is like this. Like a yo-yo, he is constantly being manipulated by his ego deficit. Persons who are dominated by deficit motivation are usually characterized by a dependency on others and an attitude of getting and consuming.

The growth process of motivation is linear as Figure 6 illustrates. Persons following this process of motivation are characterized by a sense of autonomy and an attitude of giving. The apostle Paul

Figure 6

Processes of Motivation

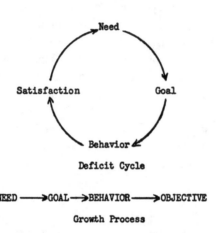

Deficit Cycle

NEED ————→GOAL——→BEHAVIOR————→OBJECTIVE

Growth Process

expressed growth motivation when he said, "I press toward the mark for the prize of the high calling." Every Christian should have the capacity for growth motivation. The teachings in the New Testament clearly advocate a caring, self-giving, creative life-style.

Before stamping deficit motivation as non-Christian, remember that God made the whole person. He made man with his physical and social needs. No person can escape being influenced by the deficit process of motivation. The challenge is to resist becoming stymied in the deficit cycle. A growth process of motivation should characterize our lives. To help volunteer leaders improve the quality of their motivation, a leader must help them find satisfying ways to meet their primary and secondary needs and challenge them to become involved in a Christian mission. A person whose primary and secondary needs are not being met can spend little energy in growth-oriented behavior.

A Look at Human Needs

Since man's needs are the source of his motivation, an understanding of these needs is essential to effective leadership. A leader who is sensitive to a person's needs can build a climate in which the person can be motivated.

As stated earlier, man's needs are both innate and acquired. Man's innate needs are his physiological needs—hunger, thirst, rest and sleep, sex gratification, general well-being, elimination, air to breathe, intermediate temperatures, and avoidance of pain. In addition to these physiological needs, man also has acquired psychosocial needs. These are thought to be acquired through a person's experience at an early age. Although psychologists differ in the way they describe acquired needs, four categories are common to most lists: security or safety needs, affiliation or belonging needs, status or ego needs, and achievement or self-actualization needs.

Physiological Needs

Physiological needs are innate needs which in some way help to preserve life and health. Although these needs are generally satisfied outside the church, air-conditioning, meals at the church, comfortable pews, convenient schedules, water fountains, and rest rooms are some ways churches relate to the satisfaction of these needs. Common sense dictates that if a church wants to engage a person in the pursuit of his higher needs, these basic needs must be cared for. If all needs of man are unsatisfied, he is dominated by this level of needs. Fasting is thought to be the ultimate in self-discipline.

Security Needs

A person's security needs relate to his desire for safety, order, structure, and stability. Because of his security needs, man wants freedom from fear, anxiety, chaos, and unpredictability.

Security needs play a large role in the church's activities. A church proclaims a message of eternal security in Jesus Christ. It is through this relationship with Christ that a person finds ultimate freedom from fear, anxiety, and insecurity.

The position of security needs in the hierarchy is also note-worthy. The basic nature of this need explains why people resist change so strongly. Change creates insecurity. The desire that many people have for a strong leader also relates to this need. The confident style of a strong leader provides security for his followers.

Belonging Needs

The belonging needs are also called the love needs. Man is a social being. Man has been known to suppress every other need in order to be accepted by his peers. The need to belong expresses itself in several forms. In early life it is evident in the dependency of a child on his parents. In the teen years it is expressed by a keen desire to be accepted by peers. In adult life it is seen as a persistent need to associate with others. One of the most extreme punishments imposed in our penal system is solitary confinement. This attests to the strength of this need.

A church is a fellowship of believers. As such, a church fellowship is an ideal opportunity for a person to find love and accept-ance. Small classes also help a person meet this need. A small class gives an individual the opportunity to develop more intimate relationships than he can in a large group.

This need can also present a problem. A small group can become so close-knit that they shut out persons wanting to join the group. This often happens because persons in the group have their belonging needs satisfied and become preoccupied with their status needs.

The increased mobility of our society and the breakdown of the home have made this need more difficult to satisfy. The tremendous growth in the number of small groups is evidence of the hunger that persons have for authentic relationships. If the formal groups in a church do not meet this need, informal groups will be started as people reach out for satisfying relationships.

Status Needs

Another strong social need is the status need. This is expressed in many forms, and its existence has been validated by many studies. This need to feel one's self a person of consequence is sometimes called the ego need. It is evidenced by the many official and unofficial status symbols in our culture. Titles and rank are examples. Status is important in terms of a person's self-respect and self-esteem. Much of a person's feelings of self-esteem are based on the affirmation he receives from other persons. However, a person needs to be able to affirm his own worth, too. By an honest appraisal of his own performance, a person should seek to develop a self-image that will not be dependent alone on the affirmation of others.

Competition has its roots in the need for status. A person or group seeks to build status by excelling others.

Name dropping and an identification with an authority figure also relate to a person's status need. A person can boost his ego by the other persons with whom he associates. Face-saving, retaliation, blaming others for failure, and criticism of others are defensive actions that stem from an individual's need for status.

Self-realization

Self-realization is thought to be the highest form of need. Maslow defines this need as the need to become all that one has the potential to become. Only when a person has reasonably satisfied his lower needs can he respond on the basis of self-actualization. A person who is self-actualized is willing to commit his total resources in the pursuit of his goal. A self-actualized person appreciates group acceptance and ego-building affirmation, but he is not dependent on them for his motivation. At the point of self-actualization, a person's Christian calling becomes very important. A person who understands his gifts and has committed himself to the pursuit of a particular mission is relating to his self-actualization need.

How to Create a Climate for Motivation

The question is not, "How can I motivate volunteer leaders in the church," but, "How can I build a climate in which, under the Holy Spirit's guidance, they can be motivated?" When viewed from this perspective, a leader's role in motivation is to be sensitive to the needs and gifts of persons, to help persons understand their needs and gifts, and to help them live out their Christian calling in satisfying and fulfilling ways. The following suggestions relate to these leadership responsibilities.

Throw Away Your Old Bag of Tricks

Train yourself to be sensitive to the needs of persons. Because the needs of individuals vary, a leader cannot have a standard bag of tricks that will provide a climate in which all persons can be motivated. Leadership should be tailored to fit the needs of each individual. A leader should get to know the persons he supervises—learn their hopes, dreams, and fears. One excellent way to do this is with the Quaker dialogue. With the group seated in a circle, ask each person to respond to these questions:

1. Where did you live between the ages of nine and twelve?
2. How did you heat your home during this period?
3. Who was the center of human warmth in your home?
4. When did God become more than a word to you?

Let each person give his response before moving to the next question. These questions relate to the development of physical, emotional, and spiritual security. The exercise can be fun, but it also will help each person to understand and appreciate the other persons in the group. If time permits, add a fifth question: How is God working in your life now?

Another good exercise is to ask each person to complete a dream sheet. The sheet can have these categories: spiritual, mental, physical, social, financial, and family. After each person completes the sheet, ask him to share his dreams with his neighbor. Then ask for testimonies about blessings that have been received during the time of sharing.

Create Team Efforts

For a person to feel that he is a significant member of the team is important. Each member of the team has a job to perform. If one member does not do his work, the whole team suffers. Teamwork gives each person a sense of belonging.

But a team is not made by simply calling a group together and saying, "You're a team." It takes effort to create a team and effort to maintain it. First, a team must have a reason for being to which all members are committed. Have each member of the

group select a word he thinks characterizes the purpose of the
group. Put the words on a chalkboard. Discuss the words and
try to write in thirty-five words or less the purpose of your group.
For example, if you are using this exercise with a group of volunteer age-division coordinators, they might choose words like train,
fellowship, share, inform, and pray. The purpose statement might
be: as a team of age-division coordinators, our purpose is to
harmonize the work of the age divisions, to dream about what
God can do in our midst, and to give spiritual support to one
another.

Face-to-face communication on a regular basis is also required
to keep a team going. Although time does not need to be wasted
in meetings, a team cannot function without good communications.
Teamwork is interdependent work. The church council or age-
division coordinating committee that meets irregularly cannot
become a team.

Teams must have openness and trust, too. If teammembers have
a hidden agenda of trying to get the best for their respective
areas of work, the effort is doomed to failure. Openness and trust
come from understanding and respect. The Quaker dialogue and
the dream sheets discussed earlier are good exercises to build trust.
Sharing concerns and praying together are important, too. Also,
try to find opportunities for fellowship outside the formal meetings.

Affirm Good Work

Each of us wants to think of himself and to be thought of
by others as a person of worth. Perhaps no single thing builds
motivation more than to know that someone we respect appreciates us as persons and appreciates the work we are doing. An
important part of a climate of motivation is affirmation. It is

easy for a leader to become so involved in a project that he forgets to express his appreciation for the others who are working in the project.

Affirmation also helps a person understand his gifts. In a recent discussion with a group of ministers of education, it was agreed that the most tangible way to understand one's gifts was from the affirmation of others. When a leader recognizes a gift in another person, he should tell him about it.

Affirmation can be public and private. When a person has attained an important goal, public recognition is justified and in order. But public recognition must be sincere and merited. If a leader constantly showers praise on one and all as a manipulative technique, it becomes worthless and even embarrassing. Private affirmation can often be more rewarding than public.

Generate Excitement About the Mission

A sedate, lifeless organization or project is doomed to failure before it begins. People want to be a part of an enterprise that is moving and achieving goals.

Considerable criticism has been leveled in recent years at highly visible promotional efforts because of their manipulative nature. This criticism is justified when the promotional efforts are built around ideas that do not relate to the church's mission. "Be-one-of-the-bunch" and "Beat our best" campaigns appeal to a person's ego but often do little to hold up the mission of the church. On the other hand campaigns such as "Strength for Living," and "Life's Greatest Adventure" reflect the real purpose of the church.

There are many practical ways to add excitement. Here are just a few:

1. Have a celebration time in the worship service instead of announcements.

2. Plan your year's work around a theme that reflects your goals for the year.

3. Have an attractive bulletin board for promoting current programs.

4. Use a midweekly news sheet to report on last week's events and announce coming activities.

5. Ask teachers and directors to give testimonies during various meetings.

6. Develop a slogan for your church that captures its uniqueness.

7. Develop a symbol that can be used on your letterhead, newsletters, outdoor advertising, and newspaper ads.

8. Develop a leader's edition of the church calendar.

9. Have an annual worker-appreciation dinner.

10. Recognize the leaders who have served five, ten, fifteen, twenty or more years.

11. Have a get-to-know-your-leaders column in the weekly newsletter.

12. Print stories and use pictures to report on events that are happening in the church.

13. Write a letter of appreciation to each worker on his birthday.

14. Provide scholarships for workers to attend training events.

15. Recognize church leaders who serve as associational or state-approved workers.

16. Have an open house for various departments.

17. Print a picture album of the classes and departments.

18. Get the local newspaper to do a feature story on some outstanding or unusual church ministry.

19. Publish a church directory that lists the names, addresses, and phone numbers of the church-elected leaders.

20. Have a teacher-appreciation day when each class will honor its teacher.

21. Take slides or movies of the work in various departments and put together a presentation for the church.

22. Have classes and/or departments sit together and be recognized in the worship service.

23. Recognize leaders and members who have had perfect attendance.

24. Designate a "department of the week." Give highlights about it in the newsletter and announcements.

25. Develop a parents' handbook for Preschool, Children, and Youth departments.

Give Volunteer Leaders Visibility

The size of an organization and the professionalism of the staff affect the ability of the rank and file to attain visibility in the organization. As the size and professionalism of the staff grow, the visibility and role of the volunteer leader is often diminished. Staff leaders can sometimes become so concerned with their own visibility that they forget the necessity of sharing recognition with volunteer leaders.

Be Willing to Share Responsibility and Authority

This is a principle of both supervision and of motivation. Few people like to be legmen. Persons want to have the authority to make decisions regarding the work they do. For various reasons it is easy for a staff leader to lose sight of this need and make all major and many of the minor decisions himself. A person's motivation will soar when he realizes he has been entrusted with decision-making responsibility. This is one reason deacons are so highly motivated. The church has set them apart by ordination and has entrusted both authority and responsibility to them.

Get the Right Person in a Job

It's demotivating for a person to be in a job that he doesn't enjoy. A person needs to feel that he can live out his Christian calling in the position he has. How many times have you heard a volunteer leader say, "I didn't want this job when I took it. I just took it because no one else would take it, and I couldn't let the Lord down." A person is done a great injustice when he is influenced to take a task to which he does not feel called.

A person may not discover his dissatisfaction until he has been in the job for a few months. A leader should try to stay in close communication with workers whose motivation begins to wane. Apathy will often be the result of a feeling of failure or boredom. If a person is not finding personal satisfaction, he should be helped to find another place of service that is satisfying. Otherwise the volunteer may withdraw and refuse to serve in the future.

Keep Working Toward Goals

A goal-oriented environment is a motivating environment. Guide volunteer leaders to set personal and organizational goals. Because most volunteer leaders are also involved in family, occupational, and community affairs, their volunteer work at the church can become a low priority. Without your help they may not set goals. Someone has said, "If you aim at nothing, that's what you hit." Goal-setting will be discussed more fully in the chapter dealing with planning.

Give Workers Your Personal Attention

Praise or criticize, but don't ignore. I recently talked with a pastor about a leader in his church who was lukewarm. Because of his cultural background he felt insecure in his leadership role. The pastor was concerned because he felt this individual had great potential and was on the verge of withdrawing. In an effort to help, the pastor decided to give the person his personal attention by involving him in pastoral visitation, affirming him to the church, and giving him other opportunities to personally identify with the pastor. The pastor reported that within a few weeks the person's motivation and his acceptance in the church had increased dramatically.

Personal attention of a staff leader is absolutely essential in building a climate in which volunteer workers can become motivated. People want to know where they stand. Even negative feedback is better than no feedback at all. Look for opportunities to discuss the work a volunteer is doing. Ask about his joys and problems. Offer to become involved with him in solving his problems.

Challenge Persons to Become Involved in a Mission

Christian service is an opportunity for a person to achieve fulfillment of his highest needs—self-actualization. Yet many volunteer leaders have not felt this depth of motivation in their work. They are caught in the frustrating cycle of deficit motivation. An effective leader should continually hold up the mission and seek to involve others in pursuing it. What a tragedy it is for so many volunteer leaders to be caught in the web of minutiae and miss the joy of being a part of the mission.

5
Getting Across New Ideas

Minister X felt the girls' mission study group should change its time of meeting from Wednesday evening to Tuesday afternoon. After all, the Wednesday evening meeting meant that the girls must miss prayer meeting. They could easily meet on Tuesday afternoon on their way home from school.

Convinced of the correctness of his decision, he announced the idea in the Wednesday night prayer meeting. He didn't mean it to sound like an edict, but that must have been the way the leaders of the missions organization heard it. To his surprise, he was challenged publicly and forced to retreat.

You would think minister X would have known better than to pull a dumb stunt like that. But who among us can cast the first stone?

Similar lapses of common sense have happened to all of us. A minister is constantly dealing with change. He works with people and organizations. Both are constantly changing and adapting to the environment. A minister is continually looking for a better way to help persons grow and to get things done more effectively.

Change is threatening. The status quo is much more comfortable. Someone has said, "Old ideas are like old shoes—very comfortable and seldom discarded." The world is changing so rapidly that the nostalgia craze has developed as a backlash. A leader's role in getting across new ideas is not getting what he wants and making people like it. A leader must help persons understand the situation, see the opportunities for growth, and develop a pattern of behavior in which they can continue to be creative and effective.

Accepting a New Idea

Persons move through stages of change as they accept a new idea. Joe M. Bohlen and George M. Beal of the Department of Economics and Sociology at Iowa State College discovered in a study of how farm people accept new ideas that they move through five stages of adaptation: (1) awareness, (2) interest, (3) evaluation, (4) trial, and (5) adoption.[18] Experience has taught that these stages are valid whether persons are deciding on a new hybrid corn or a new method of teaching. This outline will be used to discuss the process of accepting a new idea.

Awareness

When a person becomes aware of a new idea but does not know the details, he is in the awareness stage. A teacher who has heard of total-time teaching would be at this stage. He is a long way from adopting and using the idea, but he knows that it exists.

A person gets this type of information from calendars, news releases, posters, announcements, bulletin boards, newsletters, articles, and many other sources.

The lead time for awareness information depends on the nature of the event. A month lead time may be plenty for a class social, but a year may be needed for a training event at a conference center. The pace at which persons move through this stage of adoption is dependent on the relation of the event to their felt needs. A person who has been struggling to lead a group of junior-high pupils in Bible study will normally process the awareness information about a teacher improvement session for Youth teachers very quickly. He may not react so quickly to a more general training opportunity.

Interest

The second stage is interest. At this stage a person wants to know the facts about the new idea. He wants to know who, where, what, and how. Consider again total-time teaching as an example. At the interest stage a teacher knows that the method exists and wants to know how is it done and what materials are used. A person's inquisitive nature works overtime in this stage.

The needed information can be carried in flyers, magazine articles, lectures, letters, news stories. Opportunity for dialogue is good at this stage. Again, lead time depends on the person and the nature of the event.

Evaluation

The evaluation stage occurs when a person assimilates the facts and asks: "What's in it for me? Can I do it? What are the benefits?" A person may continue to rely on printed media, but he also likes to hear testimonies, see demonstrations, and look at samples.

Trial

Now a person is saying: "I want to do it if I can. I'm sold on the benefits." A person must deal with the negative forces that cause him to have difficulty in putting the new idea into practice. Again, look at total-time teaching as an example. The person has seen it demonstrated. He believes that new method will increase the interest of the learners. But can he do it? Does he have enough time to plan? Will he make a fool of himself? Obviously, provision of adequate resources, personal encouragement, and an "I'll help you" attitude are important leadership actions here.

Registration to attend an event is another side of this same coin. If the new idea is attending a Bible study, a person enters the trial stage when he signs up to come. But he has not adopted until he comes. Don't forsake him now. Many of us do not get the results we desire because we take persons only through the first three stages and fail to give them the support they need at the crucial trial stage.

Adoption

Adoption completes the process. A person makes it through the trial and adopts the idea as a part of his pattern of actions. He may not use the idea forever, but for now he feels comfortable with it.

Persons move through the process at different rates according to their personalities and the complexity of the situation. Bohlen and Beal say that the simplest category is change in equipment and materials. The second level of complexity is improved practice. Innovation (one change in materials but several changes in practice) is the third level of complexity. Change in the enterprise is the fourth level.[19]

In the church realm a change from one type of pupil's quarterly to another type would be the simplest level. A change in teaching procedures illustrates the second level. A change of teacher's material and teaching procedures would be a third level. And a change from small rooms to open room teaching illustrates the fourth level. As the complexity of the change increases, a person obviously takes more time to weigh the decision.

Learning to Sell the Benefits

The story is told about a little old lady who went into a hardware store to buy a heater. The salesman began to tell her about the permanent pilot light, the automatic thermostat, and the other technical features of the heater. After about ten minutes the lady stopped the salesman and said, "Sonny, that all sounds good; but what I want to know is will it keep a little old lady warm?"

When someone shared the concept of selling the benefits with me, I immediately recognized that I had been concentrating and telling people about the features of an event or new idea but hadn't been selling the benefits adequately. For example, I had been saying, "Don't miss the study of *Guiding Adults*, 6:30, Wednesday evening, in the fellowship hall." I'd failed to emphasize how it would make teaching more effective and more personally satisfying. Or, for new methods, I'd spent more time telling workers how to use the new idea than I had telling them what the new method would do for them.

Advertising experts say that people accept a need idea for one of three reasons: (1) to get a benefit they don't have, (2) to protect a benefit they have, and (3) to replace a benefit they have lost. For example, a church training planning meeting may relate to these three reasons in one or all of the following ways:

- New benefit—The session will help you learn how to use a new resource kit.
- Protect a benefit—The session will help you review the units that are available next quarter.
- Replace a benefit—The session will help you use the new leader's material that is replacing the existing material.

The application of this concept is obvious. When you are presenting a new idea, emphasize the benefits.

Try this exercise to learn to recognize the benefits. Ask a group to help you. Place a chair in the center of the group. Ask someone to name a feature about the chair. Then ask another to name the benefit this feature provides. Metal chair legs are a feature. The benefit of metal legs would be that the chair is sturdy. Continue to name features and benefits until the group gets the idea. Then name a new idea or church event that is coming soon. Try the same exercise. The date of Vacation Bible School is a feature. The benefit is its convenience for the church families.

Also avoid generalities in your statement of the benefits.

Don't say: "Help you improve your teaching."

Say: "Show you how to use the question method."

Don't say: "Help you grow in Christian maturity."

Say: "Help you develop a plan for personal Bible study."

Generalities have no power. They are usually trite and appeal to a person's loyalty rather than his needs.

Analyze the Positive and Negative Forces

A person may reach the trial stage and go no further because negative forces overwhelm him. Negative forces are the reasons a person can't do what you ask. A person may want to attend the training session but can't get out after dark or doesn't have anyone to take care of the children. Getting out after dark and lack of child care are negative forces.

A strategy for helping persons accept a new idea should include an analysis of why a person *ought* to take your advice (positive forces) and why a person *can't* do what you ask. An understanding of these forces will help to build a plan that will stress the benefits and seek to eliminate or minimize the negative forces.

Two possible strategies are possible, as illustrated in Figure 7. A person's present position is represented by the vertical line

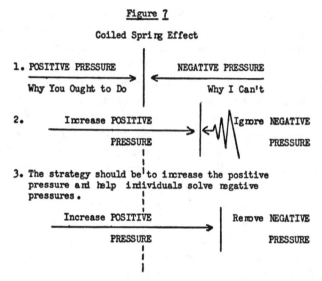

Figure 7

Coiled Spring Effect

in the first illustration. He is pushed by positive pressure and restrained by negative pressure. To increase positive pressure without dealing with negative forces creates a coiled spring effect. As soon as the positive pressure decreases, the spring will likely push the person back beyond the original position. This is what has happened when you hear a person say, "We tried that here before and it didn't work." More positive pressure will be required next time. The best strategy is to sell the positive benefits and to seek to eliminate as many negative forces as possible.

Understanding the Differences Among Individuals

Individuals move through the adoption process at different rates. Some persons accept a new idea as soon as it is introduced; others never accept a particular idea. A leader needs to understand these differences among individuals and plan his actions accordingly.

Research has shown that persons can be grouped into categories according to the way they accept a new idea. Beal and Bohlen have described the categories as: innovators, early adopters, early majority, majority, nonadopters.[20]

Figure 8 summarizes the characteristics of the adoption groups. The horizontal flow of the chart indicates time. The curved line running through the chart indicates the percent of persons who have adopted an idea at a given time.

Innovators

Innovators are the first persons to accept a new idea. About seven percent of an average group will be innovators.

Innovators are persons who are secure and can afford to take risks. They maintain contact with experts outside the community. They get ideas directly from the source. Their influence often goes beyond the community. They may serve as association or state convention approved specialists. When a new idea is presented, they volunteer to try it. They like to be recognized as the first to put a new idea into practice. They may not stay with a new idea long because of their pursuit of other new ideas. They have a tendency to get bored easily and may sometimes be impatient with their peers who do not move as quickly.

Innovators usually subscribe to specialized publications that give them the latest information. They are usually ready and willing to attend workshops, conventions, and seminars.

Early Adopters

The second category of adopters is the early adopters. About fifteen percent of an average group will be in this category.

Early adopters usually serve in leadership positions. They are likely to be below forty-five years of age. However, some older

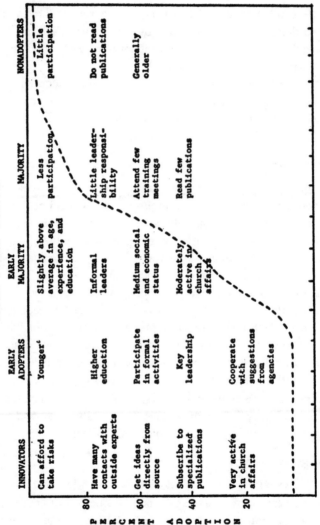

ADOPTION CURVE

	INNOVATORS	EARLY ADOPTERS	EARLY MAJORITY	MAJORITY	NONADOPTERS
	Can afford to take risks	Younger[1]	Slightly above average in age, experience, and education	Less participation	Little participation
	Have many contacts with outside experts	Higher education	Informal leaders	Little leadership responsibility	Do not read publications
	Get ideas directly from source	Participate in formal activities	Medium social and economic status	Attend few training meetings	Generally older
	Subscribe to specialized publications	Key leadership	Moderately active in church affairs	Read few publications	
	Very active in church affairs	Cooperate with suggestions from agencies			

PERCENT ADOPTION

80
60
40
20

TIME

Figure 8

persons who have kept a youthful spirit are found in this group. Early adopters also tend to have more formal education than slower adopters. They are happy to hear a new idea and are willing to try it after minimum investigation. Early adopters trust the establishment and are willing to cooperate with the suggestions of denominational agencies. They can take an idea from an authoritative source and make it work in "showcase" form. They participate in most training events. They have a cooperative attitude and will work steadily with a minimum of recognition.

Early Majority

The third category of adopters is the early majority. They comprise about thirty percent of the average group. As the figure shows, adoption begins to occur rapidly as this group gets into the act.

The early majority are slightly above average in age, education, and experience. They tend to wait until an idea is proved before jumping on the bandwagon. They are not opposed to change, but they are not risk-oriented and fear failure. Some of the early majority will hold leadership positions. However, many of them will be informal leaders who are respected for their age and experience.

The early majority will be fairly active in church meetings but will not attend many training events outside their local church. They do not read many publications and prefer to see an idea demonstrated rather than to read about it.

Majority

The fourth group of adopters is called the majority. About twenty-five to thirty percent of an average group will be in this category.

These persons have their names on the membership rolls but are irregular in participation. They do not hold key leadership positions and attend few specialized meetings. Their needs for status and achievement are met outside the church. They seldom read any publications. They usually accept a new idea by default. They go along with what the majority has adopted.

Nonadopters

This final group of about ten percent never accept the new idea. They are the inactive members of a group. They are suspicious of change and relinquish their right to participate in decision making. They are content to live in their own little world and let the group pass them by.

Application

Several applications of this adoption curve are evident. First, every leader will likely find himself in one of the first three categories. His tendency will be to work with the persons who are like him, which may cause problems with those who aren't. A leader who is an innovator will likely be too far ahead of many of his group. He may become impatient, and human relations problems may develop. A leader whose basic nature may put him in the wait-and-see category may have difficulty pleasing the innovators in his group.

A leader should also seek to relate his leadership appropriately to each type person. For example, he may ask the innovators to attend special meetings and bring back ideas. He can use early adopters to model new ideas. He can be patient with the early majority and not force them to make a decision before they are ready. He cannot become discouraged when some individuals never adopt the idea. Multiple strategies are needed to gain maximum acceptance of a new idea.

Developing a Strategy for Change

In summary, the information in this chapter boils down to a five-step process of implementation:

1. *State your objectives specifically.*—Write a statement of your objectives. Are they realistic? Can they be achieved? Do you know exactly what you want to accomplish? Is it clear enough to be explained to others?

2. *Identify the features and benefits of the idea.*—Features tell who, what, when, and where. Benefits tell how it is going to help an individual. Every feature should produce one or more benefits. Sell the benefits. Remember, people want to know how the idea is going to help them get a benefit, protect a benefit, or replace a benefit.

3. *Analyze the positive and negative forces.*—Know why people can't do what you ask. Design your program and your promotion to help them eliminate the negative forces. The best plan will emphasize the *oughts* and help persons solve the *can'ts.*

4. *Plan actions to relate to the adoption process and individual differences.*—Carefully design a plan to present a new idea and seek its adoption. Begin with awareness. Give adequate explanation of the features and benefits. Tell your story over and over again. Take into consideration that some people will accept the idea immediately, but the majority will likely come much later.

5. *Check up on your effectiveness.*—Monitor your progress. Be flexible. Make changes in the plan along the way. It's the only way the majority will ever adopt the idea.

6
Designing a Sound Organization

A church must get things done. The Great Commission makes this clear. In order to be the people of God, we must do what he commands. The mission can't be accomplished if each Christian goes in his own direction. We must work together. This is what organization is for—so that we can work together in order to fulfill God's commands.

God is the master organizer; the universe is a vivid example of his handiwork.

The Scriptures have many references to the use of organization. One of the first and most classic examples is the reference to Moses' division of the Hebrew people into groups of thousands, hundreds, and fifties (Ex. 18:21-22). Every minister can certainly identify with Moses. He was serving as leader in every area of the life of Israel; but on the advice of Jethro, his father-in-law, Moses divided the nation into groups and shared his leadership responsibility with other capable men.

In the New Testament Christ also shows us the importance of good organization. He chose the apostles and trained them to carry out his work. He sent out his disciples two by two. He told them what to do and asked them to report when they returned. This is also a good lesson in organization. As Christ sent out the disciples, he fixed the responsibility, gave the authority, and asked for a report of achievement.

Why Good Organization Is Important

Some ministers have a negative feeling toward organization. They feel it gets in the way of a church's progress. It is true that a church can have too much organization and that some people spend so much time maintaining the organization they forget the purpose behind it. James L. Sullivan, former president of The Sunday School Board, says that organization is like the digestive system of the body. "You are utterly unaware of digestion as long as it is working," says Dr. Sullivan, "but when it ceases to function properly, you aren't aware of anything else. But that is indigestion, not digestion. Now when you become aware of it, it means it is malfunctioning. Good organization is just as unnoticeable as the digestive system of the body when it is functioning properly." [21]

Here are some specific benefits of good organization.

1. *Good organization fixes responsibility.* An old saying states that everybody's job is nobody's job. When we organize to accomplish a job, we specifically assign parts of that job to different people. For example, if the properties committee has the responsibility for maintaining the building and grounds, you know exactly whom to call when the baptistry needs to be fixed.

2. *Good organization distributes the work.* It is said that 80 percent of a church's work is done by 20 percent of its people. When we organize properly, the work of the church can be distributed among a greater number of church members. This also allows us to match the skill of a person with the job to be done.

3. *Good organization pinpoints authority.* Sometimes work is not accomplished because no one has the authority to make a decision. The Sunday School teachers may want to set up a training

course, but no one feels that he has the authority to do so. With proper organization someone will have the responsibility and authority to schedule leader training opportunities.

4. *Good organization establishes proper relationships.* If I am to do my part as a team member, I must know who is calling the signals. Organization lets me know who my leader is. A Sunday School teacher understands that he is working under the guidance of the Sunday School director.

5. *Organization creates a team.* When the church's work is organized, each person has a responsibility, and the responsibilities fit together to create teamwork. When organized properly, the group pulls together as a team. Things are achieved that could never have been accomplished by people working separately.

How to Make Organization Work

Good organization doesn't just happen. Here are some practical principles.

1. *Keep it simple.* Don't set up more organization than you need. If a Sunday School class can do some special job, don't create a new committee.

2. *Put duties in writing.* Every church leader should have a written list of his duties. This will prevent misunderstandings and let a leader know exactly what is expected of him.

3. *Eliminate overlapping duties.* When several church groups have the same or similar duties, conflict is unavoidable. Energy that should be used in accomplishing the task is spent in working out difficulties.

4. *Make sure each organization has a meaningful job to do.* People respond to a challenge. It can be demotivating to be enlisted to do a job, only to find you're just filling a position. This usually happens when a church fails to evaluate its organi-

zation periodically. For example, a committee may have been needed when it was established, but now no longer has a meaningful job to do.

5. *Don't bypass people in the organization.* If there's a problem in the Preschool department, it's a real temptation to jump in and solve the problem yourself. Don't do it. Work through the proper leaders. Handling the problem yourself will likely create problems down the road. The next time a problem occurs, everyone will look to you to handle it. Also, morale may suffer because the appropriate leaders were not involved in the decision.

6. *Put your best workers at key positions.* A Sunday School department will be just as strong as its director. There is a temptation to enlist the weakest leaders as directors and save all the strongest leaders for teaching positions. Enlist the strong leader as the department director, and let him multiply his leadership through the teachers in his department.

7. *Help people see the big picture.* The only way all the members of an organization can work together as a team is for them to work toward the accomplishment of the same overall goal. It's easy for a particular class or training group to become so occupied with its own goals that it loses sight of how it fits into the big picture. We've all experienced this with classes that have their own treasurers, or become settled in a room and refuse to move even when the space is needed more for another purpose. When these kinds of attitudes are expressed, it's a good sign that the unit has lost sight of the organization's overall goals. Use every opportunity to emphasize overall objectives.

8. *Set up opportunities for communication.* An organization cannot function without communication among its members. Planning meetings are time-consuming, but they are absolutely essential to a healthy organization.

9. *Continually evaluate your organization.* Some parts of the organization will need to be expanded every year; other organizational units may need to be altered or dropped. An organization that is alive is constantly changing.

10. *Ask for reports.* A church business meeting should be a time of celebration. Church organizations should share what is happening and tell how the Lord is blessing them in their work.

What Organization Does a Church Need?

Every church must worship, witness, educate, minister, and apply. However, the specific organizations needed for these functions may vary from church to church. Each church must study its situation and design the organization that best accomplishes its mission. Figure 9 gives several patterns of overall church organization for your consideration.

Guidelines for Organizing

How a church organizes to perform its work is important. Either too much or too little organization can impair the church's progress toward its objectives.

The following procedure can be used to design an organization for a new church or to redesign the organization of an existing church. A new church, however, should begin with step 2. This procedure assumes that a minister will involve some group—long-range planning committee or church council—in the design of the organization.

1. Obtain Information About Church's Present Organization

Before recommending steps that should be taken in the future, become thoroughly familiar with the current plan of organization.

(1) *Gather information about the present plan of organi-*

zation.—Collect all recorded information related to the way the church is presently organized. Specifically, gather copies of:

• The church's charter, constitution, bylaws, or other documents that assign responsibilities and authority or define working relationships

• Organization charts or tables of organization

• Position descriptions, job descriptions, letters of appointment, or other documents concerning the work of church officers and staff members

• Statements defining the work of committees, church organizations, and other units

• Minutes of meetings and copies of resolutions adopted by the church related to organization and the assignment of authority and responsibilities

• Statements of policy and statements of procedures of the church, church committees, church organizations, and other units

In addition to collecting and reviewing these written materials, acquaint yourself with the way the church's present plan of organization actually works. To do this, review the minutes and reports of the congregation, committees, and church organizations for the past several years, and interview church officers, chairmen of committees, and heads of church organizations.

(2) *Prepare a chart showing the church's present plan of organization.*—If the church has an organization chart, it should be reviewed and brought up-to-date. In most instances, however, the church will not have a chart showing its present plan of organization. In these instances it will be necessary to develop one.

In preparing such a chart, it is important to follow recognized guidelines that will help produce a clear diagram of the present organization structure. The principal guidelines that should be observed are:

Figure 9

PATTERNS OF ORGANIZATION

Types of Unit Position	Suggested Units or Positions			
	Very Small Church (Less than 100 Members)	Small Church (100-349 Members)	Medium Church (350-649 Members)	Large Church (650-1499 Members)
Staff	Pastor	Pastor Music director (volunteer or part-time) Secretary (part-time) Custodian (part-time)	Pastor Minister of music and education Secretary Custodian or Pastor Music director (part-time) Secretary Custodian	Pastor Minister of Music Minister of Education Secretaries (as needed) Custodians (as needed)
Deacons	Deacons (a minimum of two)	Deacons (1 deacon per 15 family units)	Deacons (1 deacon per 15 family units)	Deacons (1 deacon per 15 family units)
Church Officers	Moderator (pastor) Trustees Clerk Treasurer	Moderator Trustees Clerk Treasurer	Moderator Trustees Clerk Treasurer	Moderator Trustees Clerk Treasurer
Church Committees	Nominating Property and Space Stewardship Ushers	Nominating Property and Space Stewardship Ushers Missions (if needed) Preschool (if needed)	Public relations Nominating Property and Space Stewardship Personnel Missions History Ushers Preschool (if needed)	Public relations Nominating Property and Space Stewardship Personnel Missions Food services History Ushers Preschool (if needed)

Program Services	Literature librarian (director only)	Library (up to 3 workers) Recreation (chairman only)	Library Recreation	Library Recreation
Coordination	—	Church council	Church council Preschool conference Children's conference Youth conference Adult conference	Church council Preschool conference Children's conference Youth conference Adult conference Division coordinators
Bible Teaching	General officers and organizations for each age division	Department for each age division	Multiple departments as needed	Multiple departments as needed
Training	Training director only	Continuing member training groups Leader training and new member orientation as needed	Member training departments for each age division Terminal leader training projects New member orientation as needed Director for each type of training	Three fully developed divisions of training—new member, leader, and member
Missions	Missions director only	Age division units or organizations as needed	Age division units or organizations as needed	Fully graded men and boys units Fully graded women and girls units
Music	Music director only	Graded choirs	Graded choirs and music activity groups	Fully developed music program

• Each organization unit and major staff position should be shown on the chart.

• All boxes should contain the official name of the organization unit or the official title of the position, in the case of principal positions not specifically related to a particular organization unit. Boxes for major organization units should also contain the title of the office or staff member heading that unit.

• Only straight vertical and horizontal solid lines should be used to connect boxes. These lines should show only the *primary* working relationship of the unit or position. (For example, the line from a committee box should go up to the box of the unit from which the committee obtains its instructions and to which it submits its reports. The line should go up from a staff position to the box of the supervisor of that position.) Where it is essential to show a *secondary* working relationship, use a broken or dotted line.

• The chart should be kept as simple as possible. No attempt should be made to show the many different kinds of working relationships that each position and each committee has.

• Where a reporting relationship is unclear, the relationship should be explained by an appropriate footnote.

To assist the group in preparing an organization chart to show the church's present plan of organization, see Figure 10. This provides a model on which to indicate the present plan of organization, and instructions to follow in developing the chart.

After developing the organization chart in draft form, it should be reviewed with church leaders to be sure it reflects with reasonable accuracy the church's current plan of organization.

(3) *Review general materials related to organization.*—To gain broader understanding about organization and to begin to develop specific ideas, find and study information that relates to churches

specifically and more generally to organization as such. A number of general books on organization can be found in public libraries. Books relating specifically to a church can usually be found in the church library or can be ordered from a book store.

2. *Identify Current Problems and Future Needs*

As soon as you are well informed about the church's present organization, look ahead and begin to think about steps that should be taken to strengthen it. First, see what the present problems are and then relate the present situation to future needs.

To aid in appraising the strengths and needs for improvement in the way the church is presently organized, a number of generally appropriate principles are set forth in the section "Making Organization Work." Ask: How well do we live up to this principle? How well is this special need of our church met?

A work sheet should be completed and retained for use in later steps of this part of the study.

3. *Develop a Plan of Organization*

When you have completed the review of the church's current situation, then:

(1) *Prepare all essential parts of the plan.* —Develop a complete plan, consistent with the principles of organization and the needs of the church.

The plan of organization developed should be reflected in:

• An organization chart (see *Figure 10*)

• An organization unit description for the congregation, the church council, the deacons, each committee, and each church organization

• A position description for each official church position, in-

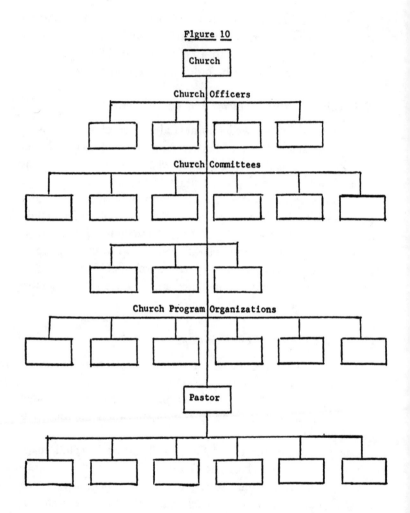

Figure 10

Preparing a Chart of the
Church's Present Organization

Instructions: Fill in this chart with job titles and names of various groups. Use another chart to show changes that may be recommended.

At this level, indicate each general officer of the church in an individual box. Example: pastor, moderator, clerk, treasurer, trustees.

At this level, indicate each major committee of the church in an individual box.

At this level, indicate special organization units, other than committees, such as deacons, church council, and church library.

At this level, indicate the church program organizations, such as, Sunday School, Church Training, etc.

At this level, indicate church staff positions. Where one staff position supervises other staff positions, show subordinate positions below that of the supervisor.

cluding each officer position, the pastor, and each staff position

• A plan for coordination, grouping-grading, and scheduling

(2) *Test the plan of organization.*—After preparing a draft of the plan of organization you intend to recommend, test the plan against the principles listed earlier.

(3) *Determine how rapidly the plan can be put into effect.*— Having developed the plan of organization and tested it in terms of organization principles and the special needs of the church, examine each change in the plan in terms of time. Decide when each change can be accomplished.

Occasionally a change in organization that will be ultimately desirable cannot be put into effect immediately. In some instances this is because the need for the change has not yet developed to the point where it is sufficiently recognized. In some instances it will not be desirable or necessary to make a change until a staff member retires or resigns or until an officer's term of office expires.

Recognize the existence of such situations. However, do not modify recommendations concerning the future organization of the church to accommodate them. Instead, determine how rapidly the needed changes can be made.

Decide when to recommend that each of the proposed changes should be made. Each step proposed should, of course, be a step toward the desirable plan of organization for the future.

(4) *Estimate the cost of carrying out each recommendation.*—Determine how much it will cost to make each of the proposed changes in organization. For example, how much will it cost to add any new staff positions and how much can be saved by eliminating others?

Stating the times when changes should be made will allow provision for them in the church budget.

4. Develop Specific Recommendations for Action

Next, develop specific recommendations as to actions that the church should take to improve its plan of organization.

As to the plan of organization, propose that the church:

• Approve the future plan in principle as a guide for future changes and actions.

• Adopt immediately the needed changes that will move the church as rapidly as feasible toward the plan.

• Adopt the changes in the church constitution and bylaws that are needed to put the plan into effect.

If the church does not now have a constitution and bylaws, recommend that the church elect a special committee to prepare and present drafts of these initial documents.

5. Prepare a Report

Now summarize in a written report the findings, conclusions, and recommendations related to organization. Emphasize the specific actions recommended by the group.

The findings you will wish to report on are those developed in the steps of the work. The recommendations to be reported are (1) the proposed plan of organization worked out in Step 3, including the specific changes and (2) the action recommendations developed in Step 4.

6. Report to the Church

The report should first be submitted to the church. Make certain that all essential points are covered and that the recommendations are well substantiated by the findings. Explain and discuss the recommendations. The church should make any changes that are considered necessary and approve the report.

7
Developing
Goal-oriented Plans

The very nature of work with volunteer leaders makes planning essential and difficult. Volunteer leaders do not clock in at 8:00 in the morning. They are not available at a moment's notice for a staff meeting. It is difficult to find a time convenient for them to engage in planning. Very often they do not find time to do their homework before planning meetings. But the irony of the situation is that these same difficulties that make planning difficult also make it a necessity. The disjointed nature of the volunteer work force makes effective planning essential if the most effective work is to be done.

Of all enterprises church groups should be the most committed to effective planning. God has given every church a particular mission to achieve. He has placed in each church the resources, some developed and some undeveloped, to achieve the mission. The church's adversary is the most cunning and resourceful competitor in the universe. And yet many church groups appear to be on a merry-go-round, doing many good things but seldom asking the question, "Why are we here and where are we going?"

Planning is essentially a decision-making process. Through planning, present and future needs are identified, alternative courses of action are explored, and the best course of action is selected. Planning helps a group to act rather than react.

Simply stated, the process of planning is asking and answering

these questions:
1. Why are we here (purpose)?
2. Where are we going (needs and goals)?
3. How are we going to get there (actions)?
4. Who is responsible (assignments)?

Types of Planning

Three types of planning are needed for any enterprise—long-range planning, short-range planning, and operational planning.

Long-range planning is planning in broad strokes for three, five, ten, or more years in advance. The number of years included depends on how accurately the future environment can be predicted. It also depends on the organizational unit that is doing the planning. Three-year planning may be adequate for a long-range plan for a women's missions organization. However, a church's long-range plan should be projected seven to ten years in advance.

The primary benefits of long-range planning are fourfold. (1) Long-range planning enables an organization to set priorities. (2) It gives the organization lead time to prepare for future actions. (3) It enables the organization to avoid surprises that make its programs ineffective. (4) It enables the organization to develop coordinated strategies to reach its goals.

Short-range planning is planning in detail for one to three years. Short-range planning translates long-range dreams into concrete action plans. Short-range goals, a calendar of events, and a detailed budget should result from short-range planning.

Operational planning is the quarterly, monthly, and weekly planning needed to implement the program. A quarterly church council meeting or a weekly Sunday School planning meeting are examples of operational planning.

The three types of planning are interrelated. For example, a long-range plan may call for beginning a ministry to senior citizens in a newly constructed apartment tower. Short-range planning for the appropriate year will outline the type of activities to be included in the ministry, make specific assignments, and appropriate the needed budget. Operational planning will occur as the various persons involved in the ministry meet to plan the weekly programs. Short-range and operational planning must be flexible. If the chosen approach for beginning the ministry does not work, a more effective one must be sought.

Volunteer Planning Groups

Many groups of volunteer leaders participate in various levels of church planning.

The Church Long-Range Planning Committee

The long-range planning committee may be a regular or special committee. As a regular committee, it will seek to develop the initial long-range plan and update it as necessary. A special long-range planning committee is dismissed when the initial long-range plan is completed. The church council then becomes responsible for revising and implementing the plan. A church should have the type of committee that will be best in its situation.

The long-range planning committee should consist of nine to seventeen members, depending on the size of the church. It should be chosen by the church nominating committee. The members should be chosen at large with different ages and interests represented. At least two members of the church council should be included. The committee will need a capable, aggressive chairman, usually a layman.

The duties of the church long-range planning committee are:

1. Prepare and recommend to the church a statement of objectives (mission, purpose).

2. Develop an analysis of long-range church and community needs.

3. Recommend long-range goals to the church.

4. Recommend long-range strategies to the church.

5. Evaluate the long-range effectiveness of the church's programs.

The Church Council

The church council consists of the administrative leaders of the church organizations and the church staff. In most churches this would include the pastor, other ministerial staff members, the Sunday School director, the Church Training director, the directors of missions organizations, the music director, and the deacon chairman. Committee chairmen and the directors of the church library and recreation staff may serve as regular or ex officio members. The pastor usually serves as chairman. The principal function of the church council is to plan, coordinate, and evaluate the church's ongoing programs of work. The council should meet regularly—at least quarterly and preferably monthly.

The specific duties of the church council are:

1. Formulate and recommend to the church suggested objectives (if the church does not have a long-range planning committee) and short-range goals.

2. Develop and recommend to the church action plans for reaching church goals.

3. Review and coordinate suggested program plans and actions by church officers, organizations, and committees; and provide for adequate communication among church officers, organization directors, and committee chairmen.

4. Review and report as appropriate to the church the use of resources in terms of the needs of the church programs as they work toward the achievement of the objectives and goals of the church.

5. Evaluate program achievements in terms of church objectives and goals, and report evaluation to the church.

Organizational Planning Groups

Each organizational unit of the church should have a planning group that plans, coordinates, and evaluates its work. The Sunday School council, Church Training council, and music council are examples of this group. The membership of these groups consists of the directors of the units within each organization, and the general officers. The director of the organization serves as chairman. The group should meet monthly to plan, coordinate, and evaluate the organization's work. The group does not report formally to any other body. The director formally reports to the church concerning the work of the organization. He also serves on the church council and uses his organizational planning group to prepare and implement work related to the church council. In reality the organizational planning group is the means the director uses to involve the various unit directors in the management of his organization. The specific duties of an organizational planning group are:

1. Evaluate the effectiveness of the organization.
2. Set goals for the organization.
3. Prepare action plans to carry out the organization's assignments.
4. Request resources—space, leaders, finances, and calendar time—needed to carry out the organization's work.
5. Coordinate the activities of the organization.

Department Planning Groups

If an organization is large enough to have department units within it, department planning groups are needed to plan and coordinate each department's work. In an Adult Sunday School department, for example, the teachers, outreach leaders, and department officers could make up the planning group. The group should meet weekly to plan and evaluate the work of the department.

Age-Division Planning Groups

In addition to organization and department planning groups, some churches have age-division groups—Adult, Youth, Children, and Preschool—that meet periodically to review the plans of the organizations as they relate to a particular age division. The principal function of these groups is coordination. Age-division coordination groups will be discussed more fully in the chapter dealing with coordination.

Principles of Planning

Regardless of the planning group involved, certain principles should be observed.

Plan from Ends to Means

Decide where to go before deciding how to get there. Means/ends inversion is a common mistake made by church planners. It is easy to become excited about a popular project that the church next door is conducting and adopt it without thoroughly considering local needs and resources. High priority needs may go unmet if priorities are not set before actions are planned.

The Cross Roads Church had a training event every year in March. This year the Sunday School planning group who planned the event decided to invite a popular speaker to conduct a week of Bible studies. Obviously this was a worthy project. However, had they discussed the training needs of the Sunday School leaders, they would have discovered a great need for updating the teachers concerning new curriculum resources that were confusing many of them. This is end/means inversion. Both projects were worthy, but the Sunday School planning group decided what to do before considering priority needs.

Obtain a Broad Base of Participation

Whether it is a decision to change the curtains in a classroom or to build a new worship center, a planning group should seek to involve as many persons as possible in the development of the plan. Involvement increases commitment. People are more interested in the plans they have helped to develop. The amount of involvement will depend on the amount of time and detail required to complete the plan.

A lesson learned the hard way comes to mind when I think of this principle. The church was getting ready for a large visitation push prior to a revival. In my mind I set a figure that I thought was sufficiently challenging as a goal for the number of visitors during the visitation week. But because I couldn't to my satisfaction break the figure into department goals, I decided to work with the Sunday School officers and teachers on Wednesday evening to make the division. So, during the Wednesday evening Sunday School planning meeting I rolled a large chalkboard into the assembly hall and asked each department group to decide how many they were willing to set for a visitation goal. When I added the figures on the chalkboard, the total was three times the goal I had set. The actual number who visited amounted to about twice my expectations. I learned a good lesson about involvement of people in planning.

Determine Priorities

Every enterprise has just so many resources—time, money, leaders, facilities—with which to do its work. These resources must be used where they will count the most. This will be accomplished only if the planning group determines priorities. Here is an interesting game that a planning group can play to sharpen their skills in setting priorities:

Your party has just crash-landed on the moon. You are about one hundred miles from the life-support station which was your destination. Two members of your group have broken arms. Other persons have numerous minor cuts and scratches. With no problems you can walk the distance in about four days. The terrain is rugged. You can carry only six items with you. Which items will you take?

1. A container of water
2. Evaporated milk
3. Moon compass
4. Two-way radio
5. Emergency oxygen tanks
6. First aid supplies
7. A rope
8. Small tent
9. Sleeping bags
10. A two-day supply of space food
11. Insulated oversuit
12. Tools for repairing backpack
13. A container of matches
14. Lantern
15. A pickax
16. Shovel
17. Flare gun and several flares
18. Combination heater and cooking stove
19. Camera
20. Binoculars
21. Map

If your group is large enough, divide into several groups of four and work separately. When each group has made its choice, reassemble and lead the groups to merge their list into one list. After the exercise lead the groups in a discussion of the difficulties encountered and the lessons learned concerning setting priorities. Help them see that the main difficulty in setting priorities is the diverse assumptions that persons bring to the group. Only when a group can develop a common set of assumptions can it develop a common list of priorities.

Maintain an Objective Viewpoint

No one is completely objective. Each member of the planning group will bring his ideas and biases to the planning meeting. This is normal. The problems come when the ideas and biases are kept hidden. The suggestions in chapter four concerning team building apply here also. Planning groups must be honest and open if they are to develop effective plans. They must learn to disagree agreeably.

A pastor in a nearby community asked me to train the church's long-range planning committee. I arrived several hours early for the conference and walked through the area with pastor and committee chairman. As we toured the church's building and grounds, the pair explained to me where buildings would be built and programs would be started. Finally I asked why the long-range planning committee was being initiated if the plans were already made. The response was that the long-range planning committee was established to gather evidence to support their ideas. It will be difficult for this committee to maintain an objective viewpoint as they collect and evaluate church and community data.

Keep It Simple

Planning can get technical. In the military, government, and industry sophisticated systems of planning have been developed.

Church planners should seek to learn from these systems but must avoid getting tied up in technical terms and processes. Some persons can become so preoccupied with technique that they tie the group in knots and completely stymie the planning process. A group should do the best it can with process and be pragmatic enough to realize there will be another day and another plan. Many plans are not implemented because the implementors cannot find a handle.

Watch Out for Tradition

Someone has said, "Let the past speak to the present, but don't let the future be bound by the past." From childhood we have been taught to color inside the lines. The easiest way to plan is to update last year's plan without reevaluating the total situation. Many church calendar planning sessions only amount to putting new dates on the events that were conducted last year. To learn from our past is important. However, to simply make our planning an extension of the past is a mistake. Situations will change and new needs will emerge.

Allow for Flexibility

The Church Training director had planned to begin a Leader Training Department during the third quarter. But due to the need for leaders to conduct backyard Bible classes in the summer, a request came to conduct a crash training program for these persons. Should the Leader Training Department be dropped? Could it be started earlier? Should it be delayed until next year? The Church Training planning group had to consider these questions and redesign its annual plan on the basis of this emergency. Seldom is any plan conducted as it was designed. New information and conditions arise that were not anticipated. Plans must be changed to meet changing needs. Planners should be mentally and emotionally ready to make needed changes.

The People Side of Planning

Not every person is a good planner. Here are some people to watch out for:

1. The activist.—The activist loathes planning. He feels time spent planning is time that could be spent doing. To him, planning is wasting time.

2. The extrovert.—By nature an extrovert would rather be with people in a social setting than stuck in a room with a group of persons who are splitting hairs over alternatives.

3. The adversary.—Some persons want to argue about any subject. They take the opposite side of the question as a matter of duty.

4. The speedster.—His motto is, "Let's get on with it." He wants to let the chairman handle it. Whatever the chairman wants is okay with him.

5. The expert.—The expert has all the right answers. There is no need to discuss it any further; he has given the answer.

6. The talker.—He may not have much to say, but you'll hear it said several times. Sometimes he talks until he thinks of something to say.

7. The nontalker.—The nontalker speaks only when spoken to. He may have a lot to say outside the meeting, but he doesn't open his mouth during it.

8. The peacemaker.—At the slightest sign of conflict, he rushes to the rescue. He soothes over the situation with the greatest of ease.

9. The general.—The general knows how to take charge and get things done. He becomes the chairman of any group whether

he is the designated leader or not.

10. The representative.—This person always represents his cause. He sees everything through the bias of his organization.

Some of these people appear in every group. In fact, everyone finds himself playing one of these roles at one time or another. These nonproductive attitudes will wreck a meeting if they go unchecked. The chairman must be sensitive to such hindrances and skillful in dealing with them.

On the positive side there are also helpful characteristics that planners need.

1. Patience.—The results of planning cannot be seen for months or even years. A good planner must be willing to wait.

2. Creativity.—A planner needs to be able to develop new ideas and put old ideas together to form new ones. A wise leader will learn to use the creative powers of his group.

3. Decisiveness.—Planning requires sound decision-making. Persons need to be willing to weigh the options and select the best alternative in a minimum amount of time.

4. Realism.—A good planner sees things as they are. He aims for the range of challenge, but he doesn't see the world through rose-colored glasses.

5. Ability to analyze.—To choose the best alternative requires analytical skills. A good planner needs to be able to put things in proper sequence and order.

6. Objectivity.—Decisions must be made from the data available. An objective viewpoint is needed to weigh the facts accurately.

7. Openness.—The ability not to prejudge an idea is the gift of a secure person. He does not let his feelings about another person cloud his vision. He looks for the best idea. He is willing to let his ideas be examined and merged with others.

8. Tact.—A good planner should be able to speak the truth

in love. He may not agree, but he respects the other person's right to disagree.

9. Cooperation.—Teamwork is needed to develop effective plans. A planner needs to see himself as a member of the team and be willing to work in a team relationship.

10. Energy.—Planning is hard work and may require long hours. The planner needs the quality of health and determination to stick to it.

A Planning Model

Plans come in all sizes and descriptions. Some are long-range, others short-range. Some are developed by groups, others by individuals. Some plans involve complex decisions and others involve only minor affairs. But regardless of the type or importance, planning is basically decision-making. The planning process includes similar steps whether the plan is short-range, long-range, simple, or complex. The following six steps present a model for planning.

Define the Purpose

Each organization should have a reason for being. This is the place to begin in planning. A church, a Sunday School, a training group, and a Bible class all exist for a purpose. It is surprising how fuzzy the basic purpose of many church organizations is in the minds of their members.

It is always helpful to begin planning by asking, "Why?" One church council meeting to plan the church's annual program of work defined the church's purpose this way: "To become increasingly aware of our relationship to God through Jesus Christ, to sustain a vital relationship to him, and to be used of God to bring all men into this same relationship."

A Sunday School may state its purpose in this manner: "Teach the Bible; reach persons for Christ and church membership; lead persons to worship, witness, and minister daily."

A mission action group may state its purpose as: "To share the gospel by seeking to meet the human needs of persons in Jesus' name."

A group being assigned a project may define its purpose in terms of the assignment. For example, a Church Training planning group may be asked to develop a plan for new member training. The purpose of that particular planning session would obviously be tied to the development of this assignment.

Identify Needs

The second step in planning process is to identify needs. Needs should be stated in terms of persons, not projects or programs. For example, to form a public relations committee would be an action plan. The need would be to improve the community's understanding of the beliefs and programs of the church. Needs should be validated by facts if possible. For example, the need stated above may have grown out of the fact that seven of ten persons who joined the church in the last year stated they did not know the church existed until they were visited by the pastor.

A good technique of brainstorming needs is to print the purpose of the organization on a poster or chalkboard. Then ask the group to study the statement, evaluate the existing programs, and suggest needs for future action.

Another method is to develop a checklist prior to the meeting. List as many potential needs as you can. When the group arrives, ask them to check the ten most pressing needs they see on the list. Put several blanks at the bottom of the sheet for adding needs you did not think of.

Figure 11

A Sample Congregational Survey Form
"What Should Our Church Do Next Year?"

Select what you think should be the eight key emphases of our church during the coming year. Then rate according to importance, *1, 2, 3,* etc. The most important items to you may not be listed, if so, make your own suggestions at the end of this sheet and rate them in the overall total.

____ 1. Stronger church fellowship
____ 2. More vital worship services
____ 3. Strengthened pastoral and counseling ministry
____ 4. Enlarged staff
____ 5. Enlarged and more coordinated church organizations
____ 6. Better financial program
____ 7. More effective fellowship with other churches
____ 8. More effective fellowship with non-evangelicals
____ 9. Deacons doing more in the life of the church
____ 10. Enlarged Sunday School and strengthened Bible teaching program
____ 11. Stronger witnessing program to the unsaved
____ 12. Enlarged and strengthened training program
____ 13. Enlarged and strengthened music program
____ 14. Stronger missions emphasis
____ 15. More stress on family life and family problems
____ 16. Stronger youth program
____ 17. Better church discipline
____ 18. Deeper spiritual life for church membership
____ 19. Enlistment of inactive church members
____ 20. Stronger men's missions and related organizations
____ 21. Stronger women's missions and related organizations
____ 22. Establishment of a new mission church
____ 23. Enlarged ministry of the church library
____ 24. More recreation facilities and programs

___ 25. Ministry to alcoholics
___ 26. More participation in political life of the community
___ 27. More participation in the poverty programs of the community
___ 28. Ministry to the deaf
___ 29. Ministry to college students and students in vocational training
___ 30. Ministry to the mentally retarded
___ 31. Greater use of the talents of the membership
___ 32. More emphasis on prayer life
___ 33. Stronger program of leadership development
___ 34. New buildings
___ 35. Better parking facilities
___ 36. Better supervision and maintenance of church buildings and property
___ 37. More stress on democracy in conducting the church life
___ 38. Better communication among groups in the church
___ 39. More adequate office facilities
___ 40. More office services to the membership
___ 41. Better food service at church dinners
___ 42. _____
___ 43. _____
___ 44. _____

The congregational survey form illustrated in Figure 11 may be duplicated and used for a survey of church needs.

Determine Priorities

When a list of needs has been compiled, they should be ranked in order of importance. One way to do this is by asking each person to assign a value to each. For example, if the list of needs has twelve items on it, ask each person to select what he thinks are the top five needs on the list. Next ask each person to assign a value of five to their top priority need. Assign four to the next

Figure 12

ACTION PLANNING WORKSHEET GOAL #_____

ACTION PLAN_____

_____

Responsibility for Planning and Implementation_____
(Person/Organization)

ACTIONS FOR CARRYING OUT THE ACTION PLAN:

Actions	Person to do the Action	Date to Begin	Complete	Resources Needed	Cost
1.					
2.					
3.					
4.					
5.					
6.					
7.					
8.					

EVALUATION:

Date	Indicate Actions On Schedule	Behind	Completed	Problems Encountered (Indicate by Action No.)	Suggest Improvement (Indicate by Action No.)

most important need and so on until all five needs have been ranked in descending order. Using a chalkboard, total the points each need has received on the basis of the ratings given by each member of the group. Analyze the points and determine the top five priorities. Don't stop here, however. Lead the group in a general discussion to reach a consensus about the validity of the rankings. Some alteration may be needed when the discussion reveals new information.

The moon game listed earlier in this chapter is good training for setting priorities. A personnel committee could not agree on the items that were placed in a staff member's job description. After playing the game, they were able to agree quickly.

Set Goals

Goals tell how much of a need the group will seek to accomplish. Goals also set a specific date by which the desired result will be achieved. Goals become targets for action. Here are some sample goals:

1. To increase the class enrollment by 50 percent by April 1, 19XX.

2. To involve all newly elected teachers in a thirteen-session orientation class during the first quarter of the church year.

3. To begin a ministry to the Brookhaven Nursing Home by January 1, 19XX.

4. For 40 percent of the church families to have regular family worship by June 1, 19XX.

5. To begin a choir for grades one–three by November 15, 19XX.

6. To enlist and train by May 15, 19XX ten persons to conduct backyard Bible classes in the Edge Hill community.

7. To begin after-school care for grades one–six by Septem-

ber 1, 19XX.

8. To have an average attendance of fifty-eight percent of the Sunday School enrollment during the church year of 19XX-XX.

9. To win 100 persons to faith in Christ during the church year 19XX-XX.

10. To involve 75 percent of the Sunday School teachers in a teaching improvement plan during 19XX-XX.

Action Plans

An action plan is a series of actions planned to reach a goal. Figure 12 illustrates an action plan work sheet. An action plan should list the actions needed, the specific dates for each action and the persons responsible for conducting each action.

Evaluate Progress

A plan is just a plan. The effectiveness of the plan will not be known until the work begins. Some goals will be achieved earlier than planned. It will become apparent during the implementation that some goals will not be reached as planned. Two possible alternatives are available: change the goal, or change the action plan.

Progress should be checked at least quarterly. For the church council, Sunday School planning group, or other groups that have regular meetings, the evaluation can come during these sessions.

8
Achieving Effective Coordination

Auto manufacturers are noted for their assembly line operations. An auto begins with a few parts at one end of the line and becomes a finished product when it rolls off the other end. The timing and assembly procedures must be carefully planned and carried out if the finished auto is to be the beautiful and dependable machine that people want to buy. Every worker on the line must do the right thing at the right time to develop a high-quality finished product. This is coordination.

Coordination is needed in all areas of life—home, church, school, business, civic, social, etc. Coordination is needed any time persons or groups cooperate to achieve a common goal. Without coordination valuable resources—time, manpower, money, and supplies—may be wasted. More important, desired goals may not be reached.

Coordination is fitting the various parts of an enterprise into a harmonious working relationship. It is having the right resources at the right place at the right time to get the job done. It is also doing the right thing at the right time.

Sometimes coordination just happens. But most of the time effort is required by the persons involved. This chapter will discuss the principles of coordination, and three primary areas of volunteer coordination needed in a church: age-division coordination, committee coordination, and church program coordination.

Principles of Coordination

Although coordination is needed at many different times and levels in the life and work of a church, certain principles are applicable in almost every situation.

Coordination Requires Planning

One of the ironic characteristics of coordination is that the lack of it is seldom detected until a crisis occurs. At crisis point it is often too late to effect good coordination. A familiar situation is the attempt by two groups to use the church fellowship hall or bus at the same time. The poor coordination is not apparent until both groups arrive to use the facility.

The only way to assure effective coordination is to use adequate planning processes. Most coordination problems can be avoided if they are anticipated during planning.

Coordination Requires Communication

Coordination depends on good communication—preferably face-to-face. Remember those Vacation Bible Schools and promotion days that progressed smoothly and those that didn't. Effective planning, and communication of the plan, likely made the difference.

Face-to-face sharing is best although not always possible. Clarification can be requested and received. Misunderstanding can be kept to a minimum. A leader should not apologize for calling a meeting when important matters must be planned and coordinated. A major reason for lack of synergy among church organizations is the failure to coordinate their work in face-to-face meetings.

Coordination Requires Agreement in Purpose

Coordination problems often result from workers not having a common understanding of purpose. This means that workers are working from different assumptions. For example, if one Youth worker believes that the Sunday evening Youth meeting is primarily a fellowship period and another worker believes the session is a Bible memory period, they will have a difficult time coordinating their efforts. Again, planning and face-to-face communication become important.

Coordination Requires Involvement of All Units

Each unit involved in the achievement of a particular task or objective should be included in the coordinative process. For example, a church's weekday ministries leaders should be involved with its Sunday leaders in the development of a plan for coordinating the program and facilities for common target groups. Coordination increases the total impact of the units; its lack lessens their effectiveness. The more the units depend on each other in achieving their objectives, the more crucial coordination becomes. The importance of coordination among units also increases as their common use of facilities increases.

Methods of Coordination

Self-coordination is the simplest method of coordination in any setting. Self-coordination exists when an individual voluntarily coordinates his work with that of others by observing what they are doing and/or talking with them about a situation.

Self-coordination occurs to some degree in all organizations. The effectiveness of this method depends on the number of persons, the complexity of a particular endeavor, and the ability of the persons involved to communicate clearly. Two teachers who are sharing a map set can usually handle the situation easily. If the set is shared by four teachers, coordination becomes more difficult. Team teaching, on the other hand, may only involve two teachers, but the complexity of the situation makes coordination much more difficult.

Standard procedures are a second type of coordinative method. The procedure for collecting and recording the weekly records of an organization is an example. This method is best for routine tasks that must be performed repeatedly. Procedures should be evaluated often to make certain they are up-to-date. Procedures can be developed to achieve coordination in these activities:

1. Collection of weekly records
2. Ordering supplies
3. Ordering and distributing curriculum materials
4. Adding names to the roll
5. Dropping names from the roll
6. Assigning and collecting visitation cards
7. Securing finance committee approval for expenditures
8. Adding events to the church calendar
9. Approving and electing new workers
10. Requesting repair of furnishings or equipment
11. Requesting special housekeeping or food service
12. Scheduling the use of church facilities
13. Requesting the use of audiovisuals
14. Reporting to the pastor names and addresses of visitors

Committees and councils illustrate a third method of coordination. Persons come together to share information, explore alternatives, and design action plans that will achieve coordination. The church council and the Preschool committee are examples. To some extent every formal group deals with coordination at one time or another. The work of the church council and age-division committees or conferences will be discussed later in this chapter.

This method of coordination is needed when various persons have parts of the picture that must be seen and discussed before the endeavor can be coordinated. A church calendar cannot be coordinated until each organization leader shares his plans. Group deliberation is also needed to coordinate complex efforts. A plan to coordinate visitation, for example, would likely require group discussion to find the best way to put the effort together.

The use of individuals responsible for coordination is a fourth way to obtain it. These persons may be volunteer or employed workers. They seek to develop procedures, conduct coordination meetings, identify problem areas, provide information, and improve communication. This method of coordination is needed only when the organization is large. An employed age-division specialist, a volunteer age-division coordinator, or a volunteer division or department director provide this type of coordination.

Age-Division Coordination

A typical church has a Sunday School, church membership training, men's and women's missions programs, and a Church Music program. Each of these organizations has departments or units grouped by age. For example, each of the organizations may have departments or units for persons in the Preschool Division (birth through five), Children's Division (first grade through sixth grade), Youth Division (seventh grade through high school graduation), and Adult Division (high-school graduation and older). For the most part the membership of the various organizations within each division consists of the same persons. Therefore, it is important that the parallel departments or units in each program organization coordinate their work. By doing so they can combine their efforts to make a maximum impact on the individual member.

These parallel departments and units often use the same space, furnishing, and equipment. Sometimes they also share supplies. Coordination of physical resources among departments or units of an age division is a crucial need.

Age-division coordination is harmonizing the activities and resources of all the departments, units, and choirs of a particular age division. Age-division coordination involves planning, scheduling, organizing, and the use of resources.

Age-Division Committees or Conferences

An age-division committee or conference is a formal yet simple method for achieving age-division coordination. When it becomes evident that self-coordination is inadequate, a committee can be organized. The committee should consist of the leaders of the various departments, choirs, and other organizational units of a particular age division. Its purpose is to serve as a counseling, advisory, and coordinating group. Much of the business of a committee will not require approval beyond the consent of the membership. However, on occasions a committee will need to make recommendations to the church council and the church.

A committee should have regularly scheduled meetings, at least quarterly. One of the members of the group should be elected by the group to serve as convener.

The duties of the convener are:

1. Schedule meetings and arrange for necessary facilities.

2. Prepare the agenda for meetings. A sample agenda work sheet is illustrated in Figure 13.

3. Serve as a guide for the discussion. A sample assignment sheet for recording outside assignments is given in Figure 14.

4. Appoint a recorder.

5. Represent the committee in discussions with the church staff, church council, and other church officers and groups.

Figure 13

Agenda for Conference

Conference Member _____

Date of Meeting _____ Time _____ Place _____

Purpose of Meeting _____

Subject(s) for Discussion _____

Background Statements _____

Present Condition of Subject(s) _____

Order of Business
1. Prayer _____
2. Reports from subcommittee and/or individuals on subject
_____

3. Items for discussion and/or decisions:

		Time
1.	(Minutes)	_____
2.	(Minutes)	_____
3.	(Minutes)	_____

4. Decisions _____

_____

(   ) Time

There are two important principles to keep in mind concerning the committee membership. First, the membership should be representative of all organizations that work with persons in the particular age division. Second, the committee should be small enough for members to work effectively. When the committee becomes too large, two committees can be formed—one for workers in the younger departments and units of the age-division and one for workers in the older departments. Also, the work of the younger and older groups might be sufficiently different to warrant two conferences within an age division. This is particularly true in the Preschool Division.

Figure 14

Assignment Sheet for Conference

Assignment for _____ (conference member)
Assignment due _____

ASSIGNMENT: (Describe in detail the assignment.)
Please do the following before our next meeting _____ .
                                                             (date)
_____ Provide copy of completed assignment and/or report
        to the conference recorder.
_____ Provide copy of the completed assignment and/or
        report to the convener.
_____ Bring _____ copies to the next meeting.

Here are some guidelines for determing membership for the various age-division committees.

• Preschool committee.—Membership includes the directors of the Preschool Sunday School department, Preschool Church Training department, Preschool choirs and missions groups. If a church has a Preschool coordinator (volunteer) or an employed Preschool director, this person should be included in the committee and perhaps serve as convener. Directors of special activities such as kindergarten and day care may also be included to coordinate their activities, policies, and procedures with the church program organizations. Some churches may also want to include a parent and a doctor in the committee.

It is suggested that the Preschool committee replace the church nursery committee which many churches now have. The primary duty of a nursery committee has been to set policies and procedures for the church nursery. The duties of a Preschool committee are more inclusive.

• Children's committee.—Membership includes the directors of the Children's Sunday School department, Children's Church Training department, Children's choirs, and missions groups. If the church has a Children's coordinator or an employed Children's director, this person should be a member of the committee and perhaps the convener. Directors of special activities such as weekday Bible study may also be included.

• Youth committee.—Membership includes the directors of the Youth Sunday School department, Youth Church Training department, Youth choirs and missions groups. If a church has a Youth coordinator or an employed Youth director, this person should be a member of the committee and perhaps the convener. Directors of special activities such as recreation should also be included.

• Adult committee.—Membership includes the directors of the Adult Sunday School department, Adult Church Training department, Adult choirs and music study groups, and missions groups. If the church has an Adult coordinator or employed Adult director, this person should be a member and perhaps convener.

The duties of an age-division committee are:

1. Provide opportunities for sharing information.—The basic purpose of a conference is to provide face-to-face communication. Not all matters that should be discussed can be determined in advance and put on the agenda. Time should be allotted in every meeting for an unstructured sharing and discussion period.

2. Provide opportunities to resolve philosophical, procedural, and scheduling problems.—Because of the variety of experience

and training among workers across the division, many differing philosophies of work are likely to exist. This can blunt the overall effectiveness of the church's program within the age division. Opportunities should be given to discuss the differing opinions and to develop common understandings.

Procedural and scheduling problems within an age division are real, too. When these are discovered, the committee should devote its immediate attention to resolving them. Problems that could be handled easily when they are first noticed have a way of ballooning out of proportion if allowed to drag on indefinitely.

3. Develop procedures for cooperative use of equipment, supplies, and space.—Many human relations problems develop because of misunderstandings here. Clear and workable procedures can greatly improve administrative efficiency and reduce problems.

4. Evaluate the need for and plan for cooperative projects.—It is a wise use of the church's resources and good educational technique to conduct some cooperative projects. A parent/worker meeting is an example. The conference provides an excellent setting to determine and plan such projects. Take a few minutes of the meeting agenda to brainstorm some projects that could be conducted jointly.

5. Plan for cooperative in-service training in proper relationship with the Church Training leaders.—Cooperative in-service training is an excellent way to develop common understandings among workers in the division. Working with Church Training leaders, the committee can identify specific training needs and plan cooperative projects when appropriate. A study of the "guiding" and "understanding" books for each age division would be an excellent cooperative project.

6. Coordinate age-division visitation and enlistment.—Each

organization seeks to enlist new members through visitation. Coordination is needed among these visitation plans to eliminate unnecessary duplication and to avoid schedule problems.

The discussion of personnel needs and the sharing of names of prospective workers are useful items for the committee agenda. The committee can assist the nominating committee to achieve a balanced and best use of the church's human resources.

7. Refer appropriate matters to the church council and the organizational councils.—Committee members should not forget that they are part of a larger coordination picture. Often matters discussed by a committee will also relate to other areas of the church program. Committee members should be alert for matters that affect persons or groups outside the purview of the particular committee. These matters, perhaps with a recommendation, should be referred to the church council or the appropriate organization council.

Age-Division Coordinators

The use of volunteer age-division coordinators is still another method for achieving age-division coordination. The title *coordinator* has been used for a variety of positions. It is used here to mean a position that is interprogram in nature, that is, the position is not lodged in any one of the program organizations. Instead, a coordinator works with two or more of the organizations in an age division to assist the workers to achieve a harmonious program of work within the division. The position is usually filled by a volunteer leader who by experience and training is qualified to give guidance to the overall work of the age division.

Coordinators should be used only when self-coordination and age-division conferences are not adequate. However, the use of coordinators does not mean that these methods should be abandoned. An age-division committee would likely continue with the coordinator serving as convener. The addition of coordinators is simply another step to take in achieving coordination. Also, to install a coordinator in one age division does not mean that a coordinator should be installed in all age divisions. The need may be such in some divisions that two coordinators are needed. This is particularly true in the Preschool Division. A coordinator may be needed for the departments working with preschoolers ages birth through three years and another for ages four and five.

It is not possible to say exactly when a coordinator is needed in an age division; but when the number of departments and units in an age division exceeds six, this approach should be carefully studied.

The following guidelines point out some of the important ideas to consider in the use of coordinators.

Age-division coordinators should work with the department leaders of all organizations of a particular age division. However, time or other limitations may make it necessary for a coordinator to work only with the organizations of an age division in which coordination is most critical. When it is necessary for a coordinator to limit his work to one or two organizations of an age division, he should be certain to maintain close contact with the leaders of the other organizations. Also, if there is more than one coordinator working in a particular age division, the coordinators should meet regularly to insure proper coordination.

Age-division coordinators report to the pastor or a staff member. In churches large enough to have a minister of education and a minister of music, the minister of education will likely supervise the coordinators. In this case the pastor should work with the minister of education and the minister of music to develop procedures for providing consultative and advisory services to the minister of music.

Age-division coordinators need not be members of the church council. Communication between the church council and coordinators should be channeled through the pastor or staff member responsible for supervising the coordinators.

Regular meetings of the pastor, church staff, and coordinators will insure proper coordination with the church council.

An age-division coordinator should be a person who works well with other adults, understands the principles and methods of the work of the division, and commands respect from the workers in it.

The duties of coordinators are:

1. Consult with department leaders to resolve philosophical, procedural, and scheduling problems.—It is important that workers across the age division have a common philosophy of its work. A coordinator is in a position to observe differing philosophies and to determine the best method to resolve the differences. Often this may mean that the coordinator must work behind the scenes. Procedural and scheduling problems can be solved similarly.

2. Assist in classifying and enrolling new members.—A coordinator should be free during meeting times to greet new people and to help them get enrolled in the proper department. A coordinator should guard against becoming a constant substitute. Substituting can become a time-consuming activity that prohibits a coordinator from doing his job.

3. Consult with department leaders to coordinate the use of program materials, supplies, equipment, and space.—Delicate problems can arise as a result of shared use of physical resources. A coordinator should be alert to potential problems and seek to solve them in advance. When a problem does occur, the coordina-

tor must determine and implement a plan to solve it. Policies and procedures are effective tools for coordinating the use of physical resources.

4. Give individual guidance to department directors and workers.—In a recent survey coordinators ranked individual counseling as their most frequently performed duty. This is not surprising since they use this method to accomplish many of their other duties. Coordinators should be available for individual conferences at the worker's request and should seek to initiate individual conferences as needed.

5. Work with the directors of church leader training and leaders of church program organizations to provide training opportunities for department leaders and workers.—Because coordinators are in close contact with division workers, they should be able to diagnose the training needs of the division. Working in proper relationship with directors of church leader training, a coordinator makes certain that adequate training opportunities are provided. Sometimes this may mean a training course in the church, and at other times it may mean the provision of finances to get specialized training outside the church.

6. Work with the director of recreation to provide appropriate services.—Many workers do not know what is available from the library and recreation services. Also, the leaders in these areas may need assistance in providing the type of service the division needs. A coordinator can work with services and division personnel to identify needs and provide appropriate services.

7. Urge department leaders and workers to participate in training opportunities inside and outside the church.—Many training opportunities are available in the association, the state convention, and summer assemblies. Often workers do not receive sufficient information about them. Through announcements,

brochures, posters, and personal conversation, a coordinator can present and interpret training opportunities.

8. Assist program organization leaders as needed in discovering and enlisting department workers.—A coordinator should keep a list of prospective workers and substitutes. When a vacancy occurs, the coordinator can direct the leaders to capable replacements. A coordinator should guard against personal enlistment of leaders and workers. He can lay groundwork, but the appropriate director should do the actual enlistment.

9. Coordinate age-division visitation and urge department leaders and workers to visit prospects and absentees.— A coordinator should not direct the visitation of the division but should seek constantly to emphasize the importance of visitation. Also, a coordinator can help in the development of a visitation plan for the division that will avoid overlapping and duplication.

10. Encourage and provide assistance to leaders in planning and evaluating their work.—Planning and evaluation are important administrative duties, yet most leaders find it hard to maintain an effective process. A coordinator should demonstrate good planning and should seek to lead department directors to give priority to planning and evaluation.

Committee Coordination

How does a committee coordinate its work with another committee? For example, how does the property and space committee coordinate its work with the stewardship committee?

The problems of coordination among church committees are twofold: how to coordinate the activities among church committees, and how to coordinate committee activities with those of other church organizations.

Frankly, most pastors and ministers of education give little thought to committee coordination because of its seemingly low priority. Some leaders feel the pain but fail to recognize its source.

Too Many Committees

Before dealing with methods of committee coordination, let's take a look at a faulty concept about church committee work. Some feel that a church should have a large number of committees in order to involve a large number of people in the church's work. This is a faulty concept that must be dealt with before considering methods of committee coordination.

Proliferation of committees makes adequate coordination difficult. Like most myths, there is enough truth to the concept to lead many to embrace it. It is true that involvement can produce motivation. However, being a member of a committee that does not have a meaningful task can also be demotivating. A church should organize a committee only when there is significant work for it to do.

Plans for Committee Coordination

Beyond the problem of having committees with no real task, every church faces the need for a plan to coordinate its committee work. Here are several:

1. Make the moderator responsible for committee coordination. Most people think of the moderator's job as simply presiding at the church business meeting. While this is true, he is also charged with developing the agenda for the business session and supervising follow-through on matters the committees considered. He calls for reports from various committees and communicates with them about work that the church assigns to them. A church could go one step further and assign the moderator the responsibility of coordinating committee work. He could do this by meeting peri-

odically with the committee chairmen. Some churches that have expanded the moderator's job have asked a layman to assume this responsibility.

This method of committee coordination works best in a small church that has only a few committees.

2. Elect a church committee coordinator. This person would work with the moderator and the chairman of various committees. The plan would work best when the pastor is moderator but does not have the time to coordinate committee work. A church with a large number of committees may also find the method feasible.

3. Form an administrative commission. The commission is comprised of the chairmen of the various committees. The church elects a director of the commission. The commission meets regularly to coordinate administrative work. Churches using this method usually have a worship commission, an education commission, and a missions commission.

4. Assign committee supervision to the deacons. In some churches the chairman of each church committee is a deacon. In this case committee coordination can be handled as a part of the deacons' monthly meeting. Although this can be an effective method of committee coordination, many churches are asking their deacons to concentrate on pastoral ministries rather than on administrative affairs.

5. Make a staff member responsible. Many churches who have a minister of education make him responsible for coordinating church committee work. Obviously, this approach could be used only in a large church that has several staff members.

There is no best approach to committee coordination. A church should use the approach that best fits its situation. Several things should be considered: Make certain that each committee has a significant job and that the members know what their responsibilities are. Have a definite plan for committee coordination. Use a simple plan that requires a minimum of extra machinery.

Responsibilities of the Committee Coordinator

Regardless of the method chosen, the committee coordinator should have a written list of responsibilities. Here are some ideas.

1. Recommend changes in the church's committee structure.
2. Work with the director of church leadership training to see that adequate training is provided for church committee members.
3. Meet periodically with committee chairmen to plan, coordinate, and evaluate the church's committee work.
4. Channel work to the proper committee.
5. Serve as a member of the church council.
6. Encourage committees to meet regularly and report regularly to the church.
7. Counsel with committee chairmen when problems arise.
8. See that each committee has a written statement of duties.
9. Help committees relate their work to the accomplishment of the church's mission.

The horse that looked like a camel because he was put together by a committee might have come out a horse if adequate supervision and coordination had been given to the committee.

Total Church Program Coordination

A church organizes itself to do its work. Most evangelical churches develop several organizations with specific assignments such as Bible teaching, training, missions, music, and church administration. These organizations have specific functions to perform which complement one another. There is considerable overlapping among the membership. Each must look to the church for its resources. To achieve the church's objectives most effectively, these organizations should coordinate their work into one harmonious program of work.

Church program coordination is best achieved through a church council. The duties and membership of a church council were discussed in chapter seven.

The church begins to coordinate the total church program as it develops the plans that are placed on the church calendar. Since the planning work of the council was discussed in the earlier chapter, it will not be repeated here. However, remember that without effective planning, effective coordination is impossible.

In addition to developing plans that are harmonized into an annual program of work, the council should meet monthly to coordinate the church program as it is implemented. Many details must be coordinated that were not known during annual planning. Each month the council should preview events planned for the immediate future and coordinate the details as needed. The council chairman should ask organizational leaders to come to the meeting prepared to present their plans to the council.

9
Improving Performance Through Supervision

Anyone who is attempting to lead a group to achieve a goal has supervisory responsibilities. An effective supervisor must continually seek to better understand himself and to be a devoted student of human nature.

Charles Schulz describes the dilemma through his comic strip "Peanuts": "Strike three!" the umpire shouts as Lucy is called out on strikes. Sitting on the bench with his manager shirt on, Charlie Brown watches Lucy return to the bench with a ferocious look on her face. Charlie thinks: "Good grief, she struck out again! That's three times so far. . . . I should say something to her. . . . After all I'm the manager; . . . but if I say one word, she'll blow sky high. . . . She's so mad now she's ready to bust. . . . I don't dare make a sound. . . . Oh, oh! My throat's getting dry. . . . I've got to clear my throat; . . . but if I make the slightest sound, she'll think I'm going to say something to her, . . . but I've got to clear my throat. . . . I . . . I . . . gulp! I've got to cough, or go ahem, or something. . . . My throat feels so dry. . . . I . . . I. . . . "

Not being able to stand it any longer, Charlie Brown squeaks, "Ahem." And just as he had thought, Lucy turns to him and screams, "I didn't strike out on purpose!" The scream is so loud it knocks Charlie off the bench and flat on his back. With his cap sideways, circles spinning around his head, and a "what hit me?" look on his face, he retorts, "We managers have a rough life."

I can identify with Charlie Brown. I've been in a thousand situations where I wanted to speak to a volunteer worker about some problem but felt I couldn't because he would take it the wrong way. Sometimes I've had the courage to plunge in where angels fear to tread and sometimes I haven't. But regardless of how difficult it may be, supervision is essential if effective work is to be achieved.

What Is Supervision?

Supervision is a relationship. This is why it is so essential to understand ourselves and those with whom we work. As we attempt to guide the work of an enterprise, we do so with our strengths, weaknesses, fears, joys, and values.

Mrs. Johnson who was reared in an eastern city and became a Christian at age thirty-five will require an entirely different relationship than Mrs. Samuels who was reared in the deep South and became a Christian at age nine. An effective supervisor must relate to each person differently. He must treat every one according to his needs.

The relationship may be formal or informal. In a formal organization each unit has a supervisor. A minister may supervise only the heads of the program organizations. However, a minister has an informal supervisory relationship to every worker in the church organization. The formal relationship requires constant and visible attention. The informal supervisor relationship is more elusive and more difficult to create and maintain effectively. Appropriate attention must be given to an Adult teacher who needs guidance, but care must be taken not to short-circuit the formal supervision of the department director.

Supervision is also enabling and equiping. Supervision is helping people get things done. Enabling means guiding a person to
plan, conduct, and evaluate his work. Enabling includes proper
recruitment, induction, training, and coaching. Enabling is providing the resources needed to get the job done. Enabling means
going to bat for the workers to see that their concerns are properly
heard and understood by the providers. Enabling also includes
communicating the concerns of the church's executive leaders to
the church workers.

In *Effective Supervision* Milon Brown describes this philosophy
of enabling as supportive management. He says that the typical
company organization is pictured as a pyramid with the chief
executive at the top and the workers at the base. He suggests
that the pyramid should be reversed, with the base representing
the workers at the top and the point representing the executive
leader at the bottom. The workers who carry out the work of
the enterprise are at the top with the supervisory leaders under
them in a supporting relationship.[22] See Figure 15.

Why Isn't Supervision Better?

Traditionally, there has been little or no supervision of the
volunteer staff in church organizations. This situation exists for
at least three reasons: faulty concepts of supervision, a lack of
self-confidence and self-esteem, and a lack of supervisory skills.

Faulty Concepts

Supervision is okay in industry but not in church.—Despite
the fact that volunteer leaders are given the title of director or
superintendent, many church leaders feel that supervision is an
industrial concept that should not be used in a church. The term
supervision seems to conjure up in the minds of many people

the idea of a boss laying down the rules and seeing that people follow them. Also, some tend to think that effective supervision requires an employer-employee relationship—I'm paying you to do this job so I expect you to do it the way I say.

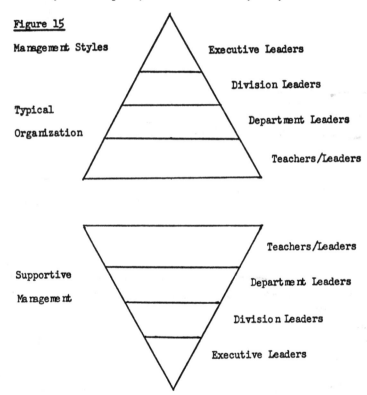

Figure 15

Management Styles

Executive Leaders

Division Leaders

Typical
Organization

Department Leaders

Teachers/Leaders

Teachers/Leaders

Supportive
Management

Department Leaders

Division Leaders

Executive Leaders

True, the dictatorial style of supervision is often modeled in industry and sometimes at church. However, this is an outdated concept and is not effective today in industry or in church. Supervision must be thought of as helping and guiding, not bossing.

How can I supervise someone who pays my salary?—Every church staff member realizes that his salary is paid by the members of the congregation. The normal pattern is the reverse of this situation. A supervisor is normally the person in the paying position. Here again, the problem is one of concept. If supervision is enabling and equiping, supervision can be a means of showing gratitude, not cutting one's throat. A staff leader should model this type of supervision and help volunteer supervisory workers to have and practice the same concept.

Lack of Self-Esteem

I don't want to create conflict.—Conflict is painful. Most people try to avoid it at all cost. Effective supervision will occasionally bring conflict. Even if you approach your supervision from an equiping stance, some people are going to be offended and threatened. This is particularly true if you are open and direct. To withstand the pain of a conflict situation requires a healthy concept of yourself and adequate self-esteem. After you have been attacked a few times, your natural desire is to crawl in a hole and forget about supervision. Every supervisor should have several trusted friends with whom he can share his hurt and evaluate his actions.

Regardless of the risk of conflict there is no substitute for effective supervision. Either mount the self-esteem to risk criticism and lead the team to the effective achievement of its task, or relinquish and try to get your point across through public announcements and stay a safe distance from conflict.

Inadequate skills

Effective supervision requires skill.—Most leaders have to work hard to develop supervisory skills. Skills such as sensitivity to the needs of others, listening skills, communication skills, and group dynamic skills are needed. Unfortunately, these skills must often be learned by trial and error. Most staff leaders do not have the training in supervision prior to their first staff assignment. Fortunately most have had patient congregations who were helpful and forgiving in the early years of ministry.

The law of readiness must also be considered. Having studied administration in college and seminary, I was exposed to many of the proper concepts and techniques of supervision. However, the real learning took place later in those "aha" moments when the emotional readiness was there.

Skill development is a lifelong task. The remainder of this chapter deals with proved concepts that if applied will make the supervisory task a more palatable one.

Techniques of Effective Supervision

At least 60% of effective supervision is understanding persons and being sensitive to their needs. However, a supervisor should know certain fundamental techniques in addition to human relations skills.

Work Through People, Not Around Them

Every minister needs this slogan on his desk. To consistently work around an organizational leader creates two problems. First, it is embarrassing to a volunteer leader for a worker in his unit to get information before he does. As a leader, he is constantly playing catch-up. He soon feels like the scout master who puffed to the top of the hill and asked the farmer, "Have you seen ten scouts pass this way? I'm their leader." A volunteer leader who is constantly bypassed without good reasons will soon ask if he is the leader or not. A staff leader must constantly be on guard against this practice.

The second pitfall of bypassing organizational leaders is the increased burden that the staff member must shoulder for the success or failure of the program. A volunteer leader will begin to feel that his services are not needed and feel little or no responsibility for the success of the program. What seemed to be a quicker way to handle a situation may turn out to be a continuing responsibility.

On the positive side many ministers find a regular time to invite volunteer workers to their home for fellowship. Informal fellowship builds a bridge of relationship across which work communications can flow smoothly. One minister of education has found that having a different group of volunteer workers in his home each Sunday after the evening service is an effective way to build relationships and improve communication.

Perhaps the most important reason to work through organizational leaders is to help them grow. This goes back to the concept of supervision. To get a new worker started in a particular job requires a great amount of training and coaching. However, as volunteers grow in their work, the staff leader can withdraw some of the support that was needed in the beginning. It is a real joy to see a person grow in his responsibility. Someone has said that a staff leader's responsibility is to try to "work himself out of a job."

Give Authority Equal to Responsibility

Jim asked Mike, the volunteer Youth leader, to plan a Youth retreat. Mike agreed and got the plans underway by lining up Bill Foster to be the guest leader. He also reserved Camp Wildwood. Excited about the developments, he saw Jim a week later and shared the news. With a red face, Jim told Mike that he was sorry but he did not think the kids were ready for Foster.

Also he had already secured Deacon Smith's cabin for the retreat. He asked Mike to see if he could gracefully get out of the commitment with Foster and Wildwood.

This situation illustrates an important principle of supervision. When you give a person a job to do, trust him to do it. If you can't trust the person, don't ask him to do the job. Also tell a person when he is enlisted if there are givens that must be followed. This illustration may seem extreme, but think how many times you have asked a person to do a job and then followed his every step to make sure he was doing it your way. Give a person enough freedom to do the job.

You also must be willing for a person to fail. A person grows more from failures than from successes. When someone fails, help him back to his feet but do not take the job from him. Only when a person can put some of his own creativity into a job can he feel a sense of fulfillment.

Clarify Your Expectations

Each volunteer leader should be enlisted by the person who will supervise him. In this way the expectations of the job can be expressed by the supervisor at the time of enlistment. This does not mean that a staff leader should not cultivate potential workers and even accompany the volunteer supervisor in the enlistment visit. But the contact must include the supervisor. Too often a nominating committee or staff leader enlists a person to accept a responsibility with the immediate supervisor having very little contact until after a person has agreed to serve. This should not happen. The immediate supervisor should always be the one to tell those he supervises what he expects.

For example, if Jerry, the department director, tells Mary that he expects teachers to attend weekly planning meetings, he can discuss her absences with her with a minimum of tension. He can say, "Mary, what's the problem? Can I help?" This approach is not likely to put Mary on the defensive if the supervisor sincerely wants to help. A clear delineation of duties and expectations at the time of enlistment will pave the way for effective supervisory relationships in the future.

Confront Problems, Not People

The most difficult situation a supervisor faces is discussing a performance problem with the worker. The discussions have a way of getting personal and painful. Such confrontations are sometimes necessary and must be handled delicately. A good rule to remember is to confront the problem, not the person. If an Adult department director has not followed through with visitation as was agreed, approach the director by saying, "What can I do to help you get the visitation plan rolling?" Don't say, "Jim, why have you folks not followed through on the visitation plan?" Also be sure of your motive. A supervisor must be honestly offering help. Just to use this technique as a gimmick will not suffice. People sense insincerity. Also you must realize that because the person is likely already feeling guilty and may be easily threatened, he may take the inquiry as a personal affront in spite of your good intentions. In this case your actions must prove that you sincerely want to help.

Handle Problems Promptly

Some staff leaders seem to follow a strategy of ignoring a problem and hoping it will go away. Sometimes it may go away, but more often it continues to fester and grow. Many serious problems could have been solved easily if they had been handled promptly. I remember a case that illustrates this well. On Sunday morning a person made a critical statement to a men's class about an action that was being taken in the church. Word of the criticism came to the minister after the morning worship service. The minister wisely postponed his lunch to visit the person who made the critical statement. After a few minutes the situation was cleared up, and a potential rift in the fellowship was prevented. The longer the problem is allowed to continue, the more difficult it becomes for the person involved to save face. Act with understanding, but act promptly.

Give Recognition for a Job Well Done

People build self-confidence and self-esteem by feeling that they have done a job well. Affirmation by others, especially leaders, is important in this process. This is particularly true with a volunteer worker who receives no remuneration.

Unfortunately, some ministers shy away from giving recognition because they feel a Christian worker should be motivated by his desire to serve God and not from a desire to receive recognition. It is true that some ego-centered persons apparently strive only for the praise of men. However, God placed in every person the need for affirmation. It is not wrong to want and get affirmation for a job well-done. As a staff leader, see yourself as God's agent. Learn to say, "Well done, thou good and faithful servant."

Stand Up for Your Workers

Nothing is more devastating to the morale of a worker than to be left out on a limb by his staff leader. Someone has said, "Stand by your workers, and they will stand by you." This does not mean that you should endorse the mistakes of a worker. But you should refrain from engaging in criticism of him. When someone brings a criticism to you, try to help him understand the strengths of the person he is criticizing. By all means, don't make an agreement with a worker and then fail to stand by it when someone from the power structure seeks to be critical of him.

The story is told about a quarterback who was in a barbershop on Monday morning after calling an unsuccessful end sweep on the one-yard line in a game on Saturday. When asked by the barber why he didnt' call the logical center-of-the line plunge, the quarterback replied, "I probably would have if I had had until Monday morning to think about it." A decision made quickly may not seem best after several days reflection. Help workers to think through the options in a potentially explosive situation. Then stand by them when the flack comes.

Check on It and Leave It There

A staff leader who picks up the unfinished tasks of his workers is building a dependency cycle that will be hard to break. A supervisor should check on the progress of a task, but except for emergencies he should leave the task to be completed by the assigned person. The practice of picking up unfinished tasks tells a worker that he doesn't have to complete the job. The staff leader will do it if the volunteer can't get to it. Soon the staff leader is so burdened with unfinished business that he ceases to be a leader.

This practice also tends to make the minister the hub of all decision-making. Volunteer workers will become conditioned not to move until the staff leader gives the signal. This makes the supervisor a bottleneck, and the enterprise will grind to a halt.

Let Workers Participate in Decision-Making

If workers have not helped to develop the plans for an activity, their vote to approve the plan may be in reality a vote of "yes, I'm willing for you [the minister] to do that." Participation in decision-making increases motivation. Also, workers will feel more responsible for the successful implementation of the plans. Involvement can be time-consuming, but the increased interest should be worth the effort.

Use Participative Leadership to Create Teamwork

This principle does not mean that a leader should not have and present his ideas. On the contrary, he should give direction and express his ideas. But he should be willing to let the group examine his ideas. He should also solicit the group's best ideas.

Lead Workers to Set Goals and Evaluate Progress

Bill, the minister of education, seemed to be fighting a losing battle. He had talked his head off about total-time teaching, regular planning meetings, and outreach visitation. It seemed that no one was picking up his suggestions. He decided to give it one more year before looking for another church.

Bill is making a common mistake. He is trying to lead workers from behind the speaker's stand with general statements rather than working individually with workers to set goals and develop plans to carry them out. One of the weakest areas of volunteer supervision is personal goal-setting and performance reviews. At the beginning of each year, lead workers to set personal goals and develop plans to reach them. At the end of the year, use these goals and plans to help them evaluate progress.

Approach the evaluation informally in a supportive way. Again, ask the worker to evaluate his own performance. Begin by saying, "How do you feel about your progress this year?"

Meet with each person you supervise. Lead him in a dream

session to set goals in his area of work. Help him to develop actions to make his dreams come true.

A Special Supervisory Problem

What can a staff leader do when he has tried diligently to help an ineffective worker improve and nothing seems to work? Any discussion of volunteer supervision inevitably gets to this question. Here are several ideas that have been offered in such discussions.

1. *If possible, be direct.* Go to the individual and have a frank discussion about the situation. Explore the problem. If the person offers to resign, accept it. This solution may not be so difficult if expectations were explained when the person was enlisted and if the supervisor does not wait too long to have the discussion.

2. *Surround the ineffective worker with competent associates.* In some situations, direct approach on a resignation is just not appropriate. In such instances, try to enlist persons to serve with the leader who have strengths that will complement his weaknesses.

3. *Move on with the program.* Often a staff leader will pull back on the program and his expectations to match the performance level of an ineffective worker. This action will only perpetuate the problem. Move on with the program. In some instances, the worker will improve his performance because his ineffective performance becomes even more visible. If he is not willing to improve, he may offer to resign.

4. *Be direct.*—When all else fails, only a direct course of action is available. Remember, attack the problem, not the person. The worker is usually very aware of his shortcomings and his guilt will make him defensive. If handled properly, strong friendships and effective relationships often come from these confrontations.

Notes

[1] William E. Hull, "The New Testament Concept of the Priesthood of the Believer," *Search*, 2 (Winter, 1973), p. 6.

[2] Paul H. Veith, ed., *The Church and Christian Education* (St. Louis: Bethany Press, 1960), p. 207.

[3] *Adult Leadership in Southern Baptist Churches*, Volume A (Nashville: The Sunday School Board of the Southern Baptist Convention, 1966), p. 208.

[4] David O. Moberg, *The Church As a Social Institution* (Englewood Cliffs, New Jersey: Prentice-Hall, Inc., 1962), p. 416.

[5] *What Makes a Volunteer?* Public Affairs Committee Pamphlet No. 224 (New York: Public Affairs Committee, Inc., 1955).

[6] David Sills, *The Volunteers* (Glencoe, Illinois: Free Press, 1958), pp. 110-11.

[7] *The Volunteer Community, Creative Use of Human Resources* (Washington: Center for a Volunteer Society, NTL Institute for Applied Behavioral Science, 1971), p. 65.

[8] *The Church Nominating Committee* (Nashville: The Sunday School Board of the Southern Baptist Convention, 1971), pp. 12-13.

[9] Ibid., pp. 19-20.

[10] Jimmy P. Crowe, *Church Leader Training Handbook* (Nashville: Convention Press, 1974), pp. 30-31.

[11] Crowe, p. 14.

[12] Ibid., pp. 15-16.

[13] Ibid., pp. 17-18.

[14] Harriet H. Naylor, *Volunteers Today—Finding, Training and Working with Them* (New York: Association Press, 1967), pp. 154-55.

[15] *Diagnosing Leader Training Needs* (Nashville: Convention Press, 1974), pp. 9-11.

[16] Crowe, p. 36.

[17] *Motivation and Personality* (New York: Harper and Row Publishers, Inc. 1970), pp. 35-46.

[18] *The Diffusion Process*, Agriculture Extension Service, Special Report No. 18 (Ames: Iowa State University, 1957), p. 2.

[19] *The Diffusion Process*, p. 3.

[20] *The Diffusion Process*, p. 5.

[21] James L. Ṣullivan, "What Organization Can Do for a Church," *Church Administration*, 14 (October 1971), 42.

[22] Milon Brown, *Effective Supervision* (New York: Macmillan Company, 1956.) p. 17.

Bibliography

Adult Leadership in Southern Baptist Churches, Volume A. Nashville: The Sunday School Board of the Southern Baptist Convention, 1966.

Brown, Milon. *Effective Supervision.* New York: The Macmillan Company, 1956.

The Church Nominating Committee. The Sunday School Board of the Southern Baptist Convention, 1971.

Crowe, Jimmy P. *Church Leader Training Handbook.* Nashville: Convention Press, 1974.

DeBoer, John C. *Let's Plan.* Philadelphia: United Church Press, 1970.

The Diffusion Process. Agriculture Extension Service Special Report No. 18. Ames: Iowa State University, 1957.

Holley, Robert. *Diagnosing Leader Training Needs.* Nashville: Convention Press, 1974.

Huber, Evelyn M. *Enlist, Train, Support Church Leaders.* Valley Forge: Judson Press, 1975.

Hull, William E. "The New Testament Concept by the Priesthood of Believers." *Search,* 2 (Winter 1973), p. 6.

Maslow, Abraham. *Motivation and Personality.* New York: Harper and Row, 1970.

McDonough, Reginald M. *Leading Your Church in Long-Range Planning.* Nashville: Convention Press, 1975.

Moberg, David O. *The Church As a Social Institution*. Englewood Cliffs: Prentice-Hall, Inc., 1962.

Naylor, Harriet H. *Volunteers Today—Finding, Training and Working with Them*. New York: Association Press, 1967.

Pell, Arthur R. *Recruiting, Training and Motivating Volunteer Workers*. New York: Pilot Books, 1972.

Schendler-Rainman and Ronald Lippett. *The Volunteer Community, Creative Use of Human Resources*. Washington: NTL Institute for Applied Behavioral Science, 1971.

Sills, David. *The Volunteers*. Glencoe: Free Press, 1958.

Stenzel, Anne K. and Helen M. Feeney. *Volunteer Training and Development*. New York: The Seaburg Press, 1968.

Sullivan, James L. "What Organization Can Do for a Church." *Church Administration*, 14 (October 1971), p. 42.

Veith, Paul H., ed. *The Church and Chistian Education*. St. Louis: Bethany Press, 1960.

What Makes a Volunteer? Public Affairs Committee Pamphlet No. 224. New York: Public Affairs Committee, Inc., 1955.